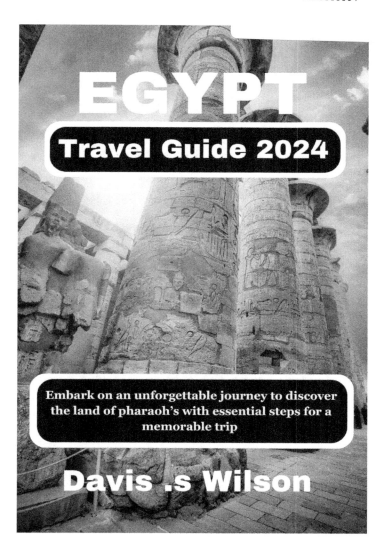

EGYPT TRAVEL GUIDE 2024

Embark on an unforgettable journey to Discover the Land of pharaohs with essential steps for a memorable Trip

Davis .s Wilson

Copyright @ Davis S. Wilson 2023

All rights reserved. No part of this publication may be reproduced, distributed, or transmitted in any form or by any means, including photocopying, recording, or other electronic or mechanical methods, without the prior written permission of the publisher, except in the case of brief quotations embodied in critical reviews and certain other non-commercial uses permitted by copyright law.

TABLES OF CONTENTS

Welcome to Egypt in 2023
Brief history
Geography and climate
Egypt people and culture
chapter 1: Planning Your Trip
Visa and entry requirements
Packing tips and essential
Best Time to Visit in 2023
Budgeting and Currency Exchange
Sample Itineraries and Travel Tips
chapter 2: Egypt Overview
A Glimpse of Egypt Today
Rich History and Ancient Civilization
chapter 3 : Accommodation
Hotels and Resorts
Traditional Egyptian Accommodations
Options for Different Budgets
chapter 4: Dining and Cuisine
Egyptian Food and Culinary Traditions

Must-Try Dishes and Local Restaurants
Dietary Considerations
chapter 5: Exploring Egypt's Heritage
Pyramids, Temples, and Ancient Sites
Museums and Historical Landmarks
Historical Tours and Archaeological Adventures
Exploring Urban Life and Modern Culture
Shopping and Entertainment
chapter 6: Nile River Cruises
Experiencing the Nile River
Cruise Options and Itineraries
Exploring Egypt's Coastal Beauty
Diving and Water Sports
chapter 7: Transportation
Getting to Egypt
Getting Around Within the Country
 Domestic Flights and Ground Transport
chapter 8 : Safety and Health
Travel Safety Tips
Healthcare and Emergency Contacts

Health Precautions and Vaccinations
Responsible Tourism in Egypt
Eco-Friendly Practices
Activities for Families and Children
Kid-Friendly Attractions

chapter 9 : Solo Travel in Egypt
Solo Travel Tips and Safety
Meeting Locals and Fellow Travelers
Travel Apps and Online Tools
Maps and Navigation

chapter 10: Language and
Communication
Essential Egyptian Phrases
Cultural Insights and Etiquette
Final tips

My Vacation Trip Experience To Egypt

My trip to Egypt was a captivating tour of a country rich in culture and history. I was enthralled with this old civilization's rich tapestry as soon as I stepped foot in Cairo.

The pinnacle of my journey was seeing the Great Pyramids of Giza, which rise magnificently against the backdrop of the desert. It was an incredible experience to climb inside the Great Pyramid, and I was astounded by these elaborate hieroglyphs inside.

Traveling around the Luxor and Karnak temples was like traveling back in time. I felt the weight of history in every stone as I observed the enormous statues and detailed carvings that depicted the stories of gods and pharaohs.

Another amazing experience was cruising the Nile River. The beauty was enhanced by the clear waters, verdant surroundings, and the sight of classic felucca boats. I went to the Valley of the Kings, where Tutankhamun's and other pharaohs' tombs had been buried for ages.

The elaborate artwork and vibrant colors within the tombs were astonishingly maintained. Amazing evidence of both ancient history and contemporary engineering might be found in Aswan's Philae Temple and High Dam.

Nubian settlements by the river offered a window into local culture, and I liked bartering for trinkets like jewelry made by hand and papyrus scrolls at the busy bazaars.

My adventure came to an end in the seaside town of Sharm el-Sheikh, where excellent snorkeling was available in the Red Sea's pristine waters. Discovering beautiful aquatic life and coral reefs was an amazing experience.

My trip was enhanced by Egypt's delicious cuisine, particularly the koshari and falafel dishes, and its friendly welcome. The perfect fusion of culture, history, and scenic beauty made my trip to Egypt one I will never forget. I came away from this trip with a greater respect for this amazing nation and its enduring assets.

Welcome To Egypt

Greetings from Egypt, a country whose history, culture, and scenic splendor are masterfully woven together from the past and present. You'll go on a voyage through time as soon as you step foot in Egypt, uncovering the secrets of one of the most fascinating civilizations in history.

The energetic capital of Cairo extends a warm welcome to you. The noises of daily life fill the busy streets, while famous sites like the Great Pyramids of Giza are proudly visible in the distance. Built more than 4,500 years ago, these enormous constructions offer evidence of the ancient Egyptians' inventiveness ,Egypt's lifeblood, the Nile River, flows through the nation, supporting ancient towns and verdant oases. The ancient Egyptian open-air museums of Luxor and Karnak, with their massive sculptures, elaborate hieroglyphs, and temple ruins, hold the key to unlocking their mysteries. Pharaohs slumber in the Valley of the Kings, where elaborate tombs conceal tales just waiting to be discovered.

Travel to Aswan to see the High Dam and the majestic Philae Temple, which combine ancient beauty with cutting-edge engineering. Nubian villages may be seen as you sail down the Nile, providing you with a glimpse into traditional life and an opportunity to partake in the hospitality of the locals.

There is more to Egypt than just the desert and the Nile. Travel to Sharm el-Sheikh on the Red Sea coast, where you can discover bright coral reefs and other underwater delights in crystal-clear seas. In this underwater paradise, diving and snorkeling are once-in-a-lifetime adventures.

Egypt's food is a delicious blend of flavors, ranging from hearty dishes like falafel and koshari to spicy peppers. The vibrant bazaars entice visitors with a wide selection of mementos, including beautiful jewelry, papyrus scrolls, and delicate handicrafts.

Egypt offers visitors a voyage of wonder and discovery because of its distinctive fusion of history, culture, and scenic beauty. Egypt's warm embrace awaits you, inviting you to write your own chapter in its illustrious history as you marvel at its ancient wonders, unwind on immaculate beaches, or indulge in mouthwatering food. Savor your journey in this ephemeral place where history abounds.

A Brief History Of Egypt

Egypt is one of the oldest and most significant civilizations in the world, with a history spanning more than 5,000 years. Egypt's history is a tapestry of amazing accomplishments and cultural contributions, spanning from the banks of the Nile to the Pharaohs' reign and the contemporary nation-state.

Historical Egypt

The Old Kingdom, which started in 3100 BCE with the unification of Upper and Lower Egypt, is considered the beginning of Egyptian history. During this time, colossal constructions like the Great Pyramids were built to house pharaohs in their tombs. The ancient Egyptians created a sophisticated writing system using hieroglyphs and constructed a religion based on gods such as Ra, Isis, and Osiris.

The New Kingdom and Empire: Egypt became a part of the New Kingdom in 1550 BCE, during which time it expanded and magnificent temples and tombs were built in locations such as Luxor and Karnak. Egypt became a strong kingdom during the rule of pharaohs such as Thutmose III and Ramses II. With the worship of the sun deity Aten, there was a temporary conversion to monotheism during Akhenaten's reign.

Conquest and Invasions: Throughout the ages, Egypt experienced both conquest and invasion. Egypt was ruled by the Greeks, Romans, and Persians in turn. Following the arrival of Alexander the Great in 332 BCE, the Ptolemaic Kingdom was established, with the renowned Cleopatra serving as its final monarch. After Egypt became a province of Rome in 30 BCE, there were more cultural interactions.

The Byzantine and Islamic Eras: Egypt joined the Byzantine Empire around the fourth century CE. The seventh-century Arab-Muslim conquest, however, brought about a profound change in both culture and religion. Islam emerged as the predominant religion, and Egypt became a hub for Islamic learning and culture.

Egypt was dominated by the Islamic Fatimid Dynasty and the Mamluk Sultanate during the Middle Ages, with Cairo serving as a major hub of both culture and power. Magnificent mosques were built during this time, such as the Al-Azhar Mosque, which is home to one of the oldest colleges in the world.

Influence of the Ottoman Empire and Europe: Egypt joined the Ottoman Empire in 1517, and Ottoman rule persisted there until the early 19th century. European countries become more and more involved in Egyptian affairs, particularly France and Britain. Egypt's strategic significance increased with the 19th-century development of the Suez Canal.

Egypt in the modern era: Egypt was under British protectorate rule from 1882 to 1952. The 1952 Revolution, which ended the monarchy and gave rise to Gamal Abdel Nasser, was sparked by Egyptian nationalism and a yearning for independence. An influential chapter in the history of contemporary Egypt was written by

Nasser with the nationalization of the Suez Canal and his leadership of the Non-Aligned Movement.

Egypt in the modern era: Egypt's political and cultural development continued. Normalization of relations with Israel was brought about by the Camp David Accords in 1978, and the killing of Anwar Sadat in 1981 marked the beginning of Hosni Mubarak's almost 30-year dictatorship. Following the 2011 Egyptian Revolution, Mohamed Morsi, a member of the Muslim Brotherhood, was elected to replace Mubarak.

Still, political unrest continued, and in 2013 the military intervened.

Egypt is a republic now, with a vibrant and diversified society and a rich cultural history that still has an impact on the entire world. Its history is proof of the lasting influence of a bygone era that continues to shape both the national identity and world history.

Geography And Climate

Egypt has a climate and topography that are both fascinating and varied. Egypt, which is in the northeastern region of Africa, is best known for its parched deserts that are dotted with the rich Nile River valley, which has had a significant impact on the history and civilization of the nation.

Known as the "lifeblood of Egypt," the Nile River meanders northward through the nation, forming a slender yet verdant and highly productive agricultural strip of land. The bulk of Egypt's population lives in this lush delta region, which also supports the country's economy and agricultural sector.

The Sahara Desert, which is significantly larger, dominates the scenery to the west, while the huge Arabian Desert reaches out to the east. The vast majority of Egypt's terrain is shaped by these dry deserts, with their tall dunes and desolate stretches.

The majority of Egypt experiences sweltering summers and moderate winters due to its desert climate.

Coastal regions, including those along the Red and Mediterranean Seas, see higher rainfall and milder temperatures due to a more moderate Mediterranean climate. On the other hand, the inland desert regions endure drastically different temperatures throughout the year.

In the summer, daily highs can reach above 100°F (40°C), and at night, the temperature drops considerably.

Overall, Egypt's distinctive climate, rich history, and need on the waters of the Nile for survival have all been influenced by the country's extraordinary topography, which combines a large desert expanse with a fertile Nile Valley.

Egypt People And Culture

Egypt's people and culture are a lively tapestry that combines a long history, a wide range of customs, and a strong sense of self. Egypt is the most populous country in the Arab world, home to nearly 100 million people, and its culture is a reflection of its complicated and lengthy past.

People: Egyptians are renowned for being hospitable and friendly. Arabic is the official language, and the majority of people are of Arab ethnicity. Egypt's vibrant metropolis, Cairo, is home to one of the world's densest populations and serves as a symbol of the country's diversity. Egypt is home to a number of ethnic and religious minorities, including Bedouins, Nubians, and Coptic Christians, in addition to the country's majority Arab population. The culture of the country gains depth and complexity from this diversity.

Religion: Sunni Muslims make up the bulk of the people of Egypt, where Islam is the most common religion. Islamic conventions have an impact on the legal system, social norms, and religious practices, among other facets of daily life. One of the oldest Christian communities in the world, the Coptic Christians make up a sizable religious minority, and their customs and holidays are an essential part of Egypt's cultural fabric.

Egypt's history and legacy bear witness to the resilience of its culture. The Great Pyramids, the

Sphinx, the temples of Luxor and Karnak, and other historic sites are among the nation's most well-known attractions.

These ancient monuments provide insights into the amazing technical and architectural achievements of ancient Egypt. They are dated back thousands of years. People all throughout the world are still inspired and in awe of the Pharaohs' legacy. Literature and Art: There is a long history of Egyptian literature and art. One of the earliest writing systems in history, Egyptian hieroglyphics have had a significant influence on historical and linguistic studies. Notable authors from Egypt's contemporary literature include Naguib Mahfouz, the 1988 Nobel Prize winner in Literature.

food: The flavors and ingredients in Egyptian food are wonderfully blended. Bread, rice, beans, and an assortment of veggies, herbs, and spices are typical ingredients. Street dishes like falafel and koshari, which is a mixture of rice, pasta, lentils, and tomato sauce, are also popular. There are also delicious meat dishes in the cuisine, like grilled lamb and kebabs.

Traditions and Festivals: Egyptians observe a variety of secular and religious holidays. The two main Islamic festivals are Eid al-Fitr and Eid al-Adha, while Coptic Christians celebrate Christmas and Easter. Celebrated annually by individuals of all origins, "Sham el-Nessim" is a springtime celebration characterized by picnics and vibrant customs.

Music and Dancing: The oud and qanun are two distinctive instruments that define traditional Egyptian music. The captivating art of belly dancing, which frequently accompanies live music performances, is another well-known export from the nation. Egyptian music today is characterized by a vibrant musical landscape that combines traditional and modern elements. Egypt's people and culture are a fascinating blend of traditional customs and contemporary influences. Egypt is a fascinating and vibrant destination for culture because of its dynamic and diversified civilization, which is constantly changing while keeping a strong link to its historical roots.

Chapter 1:
Planning Your Trip

Arranging a journey to Egypt is a thrilling undertaking that demands meticulous planning to guarantee a seamless and unforgettable experience. Here are some crucial actions to think about:

1. Investigation and Route:

Start by learning about the most popular sights in Egypt, such as the Red Sea resorts, the Great Pyramids, and the temples of Luxor. To gain an idea of the locations you wish to see and the length of your stay, make a preliminary itinerary.

2. Documentation and Visa:

Verify the visa requirements for Egypt based on your nationality, and make sure your passport is valid for a minimum of six months from the date of your intended visit.

3. The Ideal Time to Go: Take Egypt's weather into account. Red Sea viewing is excellent in the spring and fall, while seeing historic sites is best done in the cooler months of November through February.

4. Immunizations and Health-Related Planning:

For advice on recommended vaccinations, such as those for typhoid and hepatitis A, consult a medical practitioner. To cover unforeseen medical costs, think about purchasing travel insurance.

5. Lodging: Reserve lodging well in advance, particularly in well-known tourist destinations like Cairo, Luxor, and Sharm el-Sheikh. There are several options, from opulent resorts to affordable hostels.

6. Packing: Bring comfortable walking shoes, sunscreen, a hat, and light, breathable clothing. When visiting places of worship, dress modestly by covering your knees and shoulders.

7. Money and Currency: The Egyptian Pound (EGP) is the currency. Carrying both cash and credit cards is advised. ATMs are widely accessible.

8. Safety Measures : Keep yourself updated on Egypt's political and security conditions, and heed travel recommendations. Use reliable transportation services and use caution with your possessions.

9. Language and Communication: Although English is widely spoken by Egyptians in tourist areas, Arabic remains the official language. Acquiring a few fundamental Arabic phrases can be beneficial.

10. Local customs and cuisine: Learn about Egyptian cuisine, which includes delicacies like falafel and koshari. Recognize regional traditions, such as wearing modest clothing when visiting places of worship.

11. Guided Tours vs. Independent Travel: Choose the type of travel you like best—independent or guided. Each has benefits of its own; guided tours offer insights from experienced guides.

12. Gifts and Souvenirs: Egypt provides exclusive gifts and souvenirs, such as jewelry, fragrances, and papyrus art. In markets, haggling is commonplace, so be ready to bargain.

You may arrange a well-rounded vacation to Egypt that will enable you to take in its historical treasures, respect its culture, and relish the one-of-a-kind experiences this intriguing nation has to offer by following these guidelines and being adaptable with your plans.

Visa and Entry Requirements

It's important to know the entry and visa requirements before visiting Egypt, as they can change based on your nationality. A summary of the standard protocols is provided below:

1. Visa Types: Egypt provides a variety of visas, such as business, transit, and tourist visas. For most travelers, a tourist visa is necessary.

2. Visa on Arrival (VoA): Citizens of specific nations are eligible for visas on arrival in Egypt. It is advisable to verify the length permitted, the expenses associated, and whether your nationality qualifies for VoA. VoA is usually issued at some land border crossings and the main international airports.

3. E-Visa: Egypt also offers an online visa application system that enables you to apply for a visa in advance of your travels. With this option, you may conveniently check the status of your application online and acquire your visa ahead of time.

4. Consular Visa: You may occasionally need to submit an application for a visa at the Egyptian embassy or consulate in your nation of residence. Verify the particular specifications and turnaround times applicable to your area.

5. Visa Fees: The cost of a visa varies based on your country, the kind of visa, and the mode of application (consular, e-visa, or VoA). When applying, make sure you review the most recent pricing schedule.

6. Validity of Passport: Your passport must be valid for a minimum of six months after the date of your intended departure from Egypt.

7. Visa Extensions: You can frequently ask for a visa extension at the Egyptian Passport and Immigration Authority if you're in Egypt and would like to stay longer.

It's important to confirm the most recent information with the Egyptian embassy or consulate in your home country or on their official website prior to your travel, as entrance criteria and rules are subject to change. Respecting these guidelines can help guarantee a trouble-free and delightful trip to Egypt, a nation with a fascinating history and breathtaking sights.

Packing Tips And Essential

Take into account Egypt's temperature, culture, and the variety of activities you plan to partake in when packing for your trip there. Here are some crucial pointers for packaging:

1. Lightweight Clothes: Because Egypt has a hot desert climate, bring clothes that are breathable and light, like cotton. Make sure to pack modest apparel for trips to places of worship.

2. Sun Protection: To shield oneself from the intense Egyptian sun, wear a wide-brimmed hat, sunglasses, and sunscreen.

3. Comfy Shoes: If you intend to visit historical locations, you should definitely wear comfortable walking shoes. Shoes with closed toes are advised for trips into the desert.

4. Electrical Adapters: Type C and Type F outlets are used in Egypt. Bring the right adapters for the electronics you own.

5. Medication: Make sure you have enough prescription medication with you for the trip. Bringing a basic medical kit with necessary items like painkillers and stomach pills is also a smart idea.

6. Travel Documents: Remember to include printed copies of your itinerary and hotel reservations, together with your passport, visa, and travel insurance.

7. Cash and Cards: Bring cash and credit/debit cards in various amounts of Egyptian Pounds. Although there are plenty of ATMs, it's a good idea to have some local cash on hand.

8. Travel Accessories: To keep your valuables safe, think about investing in a neck pouch or money belt. For your travels, a daypack, a reusable water bottle, and a universal plug adaptor are useful extras.

9. Toiletries: While standard toiletries are available, you may find it more convenient to bring your own basics, including any particular personal hygiene products.

10. Entertainment: A book, e-reader, or other kind of entertainment may make long trips or downtime more pleasurable.

11. Camera and Accessories: Use your smartphone's camera or camera to take pictures of the amazing landscape and historical sites. Remember to bring spare memory cards and charging supplies.

12. Local Currency: Get some cash exchanged at the airport or in your own country to cover your initial travel expenses.

Keep in mind that Egypt's weather can change based on the season and the area you're visiting.

Prior to your journey, always check the weather prediction and modify your packing list as necessary. Being organized will make your trip to Egypt, with its rich history and breathtaking scenery, more pleasant and pleasurable.

Best Time To Visit

Egypt has many seasons, so the ideal time to visit will rely heavily on your interests and the activities you want to do. Here's a summary of the best seasons for various travel experiences in 2023 and 2024:

1. Fall: Generally speaking, October through November is the ideal season to travel to Egypt. It's a delightfully warm day, ideal for touring ancient monuments such as Luxor, Aswan, and the Pyramids. This is the best time of year for the Nile cruises.

2. Winter (December to February): Egypt's warmer winters are ideal for exploring the country's history and culture. It's pleasant to spend time outdoors during the day, and evenings can be chilly, particularly in the desert. During this season, diving and snorkeling along the Red Sea shore are also very popular.

3. Spring (March to May): With mild temperatures and a beautiful landscape, spring is another fantastic season to visit Egypt. It's perfect for touring historical places and taking in the scenery. Several Coptic Christian festivals take place at this time, including Easter, a prominent Christian holiday.

4. Summer, which runs from June to August: This is the hottest and driest season, but it's also the busiest travel time of year. You can still have a good time during your stay, provided you can withstand the extreme temperatures.

This is a popular season to visit the Red Sea resorts, which provide great water sports.

Take your tastes into consideration while determining the ideal time to travel. Save your plans for spring or fall if you wish to avoid the excessive heat. The Red Sea is great for diving all year round, but if you want a busier vibe, think about visiting in the summer. Winter might be the ideal option if the historical and cultural aspects are more interesting to you.

It is advisable to refer to the most recent travel warnings and be informed about any noteworthy occasions or celebrations that could impact your itinerary. Egypt offers wonderful experiences all year round, regardless of when you choose to visit, thanks to its rich history, breathtaking scenery, and vibrant culture.

Budgeting And Currency Exchange

A seamless and economical vacation to Egypt requires planning a budget and being aware of currency conversion. Here's a financial management handbook to aid you while in Egypt:

1. Create a Budget: Prior to your journey, create a budget that details the costs you anticipate incurring for lodging, transportation, meals, entertainment, and mementos. Having a well-defined budget will facilitate monitoring your expenses.

2. Lodging: Egypt provides a variety of lodging choices to accommodate a range of price points. There are upscale accommodations, moderately priced hotels, and inexpensive hostels. Make a budget that takes your comfort level into account.

3. mobility: Public buses and taxis are reasonably priced forms of local mobility. Buses or domestic planes are your options for lengthier trips between cities. Make advance plans for your transportation costs.

4. Food and Dining: Egyptian food is available for both expensive restaurants and street food that is reasonably priced. Not only are street foods like koshari and falafel tasty, but they're also reasonably priced. Putting money aside to dine at neighborhood eateries is a terrific way to experience real cuisines.

5. Activities and Sightseeing: Museum and historical site admission costs can mount up. Make travel plans and budget for these sites. Seniors and students sometimes receive discounts from historical places, so be sure to bring appropriate identification.

6. Exchange of Currency: The Egyptian Pound (EGP) is the currency used locally. It's a good idea to have a variety of cash on hand and utilize credit or debit cards for bigger purchases. Even while ATMs are widely available in larger cities, it's a good idea to carry cash on hand in case of unforeseen expenses or for smaller, more remote purchases.

7. Exchange Rates: It's important to monitor exchange rates because they can alter. Since local banks and official exchange offices usually provide higher rates than airports or hotels, it is usually best to convert currency there. To prevent card problems, let your bank know about your travel schedule as well.

8. Bargaining: It is normal to engage in bargaining in Egyptian markets and bazaars.

Because haggling is a necessary part of the shopping experience, be ready to get cheaper pricing.

9. Tipping: In Egypt, especially in the service sector, it is common to leave a gratuity. Tip restaurant servers, tour guides, and hotel employees with consideration. For this use, keep small denominations of EGP.

10. Safety and Security: To reduce the chance of theft and keep your possessions safe, carry a money belt or pouch. Use caution when accessing ATMs, and keep big amounts of cash out of sight.

You may have fun in Egypt and properly manage your spending by using a variety of payment options, keeping an eye on foreign exchange rates, and creating a sensible budget. Amazing historical, cultural, and environmental adventures can be had in Egypt, and making the most of your trip is ensured by careful budgeting.

Sample itineraries And Travel Tips

1. Traditional Egypt Tour (7–10 Days):

Days 1–3: Cairo, Egypt Museum, Sphinx, Pyramids. **Days 4-5:** Visit the Luxor Temples and Karnak.

Days 6-7: Come to Aswan, see the High Dam, Philae Temple, and take a Nile cruise.

Days 8–10: Spend time relaxing and having fun in the water at the Red Sea (Sharm el-Sheikh or Hurghada).

2. Nile Cruise and History (5-7 Days): Visit Cairo, the Pyramids, the Sphinx, and the Museum on Days 1-3.

Days 4–7: Take a Nile boat from Luxor to Aswan, stopping along the way to see villages, temples, and tombs.

Travel Advice:

1. Honor Local Customs: Wear modest clothing, particularly when visiting places of worship. Additionally, it's polite to get someone's permission before taking their picture.

2. Drink plenty of water: The desert climate can be quite dry. Drink lots of water and have a reusable bottle with you.

3. Trade tiny Bills: Save tiny amounts of Egyptian Pounds for modest transactions and gratuities.

4. Bargain Skillfully: Bargaining is normal in markets. Be ready to haggle and start at a cheaper price.

5. Remain Informed: Prior to your journey, check travel warnings and keep up with local news.

6. Use Reputable Services: For your comfort and safety, pick reputable tour companies and transportation companies.

7. Acquire Some Basic Arabic Phrases: Even though English is widely used in Egypt, knowing a few Arabic terms will improve your trip.

8. Taste Local Food: To experience real flavors, try street sellers' offerings of Egyptian cuisine like falafel and koshari.

9. Tipping: It's common to leave a tip. Keep little money on hand to leave tips for guides, waiters, and hotel employees.

10. Show Environmental Respect: Egypt's historical sites are priceless. Keep artifacts safe by avoiding touching or climbing on them.

Egypt provides a multitude of cultural and historical experiences. These pointers can assist you in making the most of your trip while honoring regional customs and traditions, whether you want to travel a traditional itinerary or take a cruise around the Nile.

Chapter 2:
Overview Of Egypt

At the meeting point of Africa and the Middle East, Egypt is a timeless country with a history as varied and rich as the colors of the Nile.

This nation, with its compelling fusion of culture, history, and scenic beauty, is steeped in both ancient mystique and contemporary vibrancy.

The great Nile River, which has supported life in this desert nation for millennia, is fundamental to Egypt. Egypt's agricultural success is largely due to the fertile Nile Delta and the surrounding desert.

The vast river flows through ancient towns such as Cairo, Luxor, and Aswan.

There is no historical significance like that of Egypt. Archaeological marvels abound, ranging from the colossal Pyramids of Giza to the temples of Luxor and Karnak.

Visitors are enthralled by the Sphinx's charm, and the Valley of the Kings contains the pharaohs' secrets. Egypt in the modern era is a vibrant mosaic of life. The Red Sea resorts of Sharm el-Sheikh and Hurghada provide world-class diving and sun-soaked leisure, while Cairo, the capital, is a bustling city.

Every visit is a gastronomic adventure because of the delicious food, which includes falafel and koshari, as well as the friendly welcome of the locals.

Centuries-old contributions to Egypt's music, art, and literature continue to flourish the country's culture.

The majority religion is Islam, but the country is diverse with a large Christian Coptic community as well as Nubian and Bedouin traditions. Arabic is the official language.

Egypt is a country full of contradictions and differences, where the vitality of a contemporary nation coexists with the ageless echoes of history. Travelers are still enthralled with this site because it provides a singular and remarkable trip across the ages.

A Glimpse Of Egypt Today

Egypt today offers an intriguing fusion of energetic modernism, colorful culture, and ancient history. Cairo, the vibrant capital, is a vast city with a mix of modern buildings and historic markets. The sounds of passing vehicles and the odors of street food vendors fill the city's streets.

The Nile River continues to be the lifeblood of the nation, as cruise ships transport tourists to important historical sites and felucca boats float through its timeless waters.

Travelers from all over the world are drawn to the Great Pyramids of Giza, which stand like enduring sentinels against the backdrop of the desert.

The thriving Red Sea resorts of Sharm el-Sheikh and Hurghada, located in contemporary Egypt, entice visitors with their immaculate beaches and top-notch diving.

The nation's pulse is echoed by traditional music, such as the captivating sounds of the oud. Although the majority religion is Islam and Arabic is the official language, Egypt is a multicultural country that welcomes Christians, Nubians, and Bedouins, each of whom contributes distinctive cultural components.

Flavors such as koshari, falafel, and fragrant teas entice the senses.

Egypt, however, faces modern difficulties, such as those pertaining to the economy, education, and infrastructure. The political climate of the nation has changed as a result of recurring elections and changes.

Egypt is a fascinating location for tourists wanting to experience its diverse culture, historical treasures, and the lively spirit of its people because it presents a fascinating contrast between its ancient legacy and a fast growing current.

Rich History And Ancient Civilization

For millennia, the world has been captivated by Egypt's rich history and ancient civilization, leaving a lasting legacy that has had a significant impact on human culture and comprehension.

Here's a look at this incredible historical voyage: Approximately 3100 BCE to 30 BCE: Around 3100 BCE, Pharaoh Narmer united Upper and Lower Egypt, marking the beginning of Egypt's history.

This signaled the beginning of one of the oldest and most persistent civilizations in history. Egypt's great accomplishments, such as its colossal buildings, architectural marvels, and intricate hieroglyphic writing system, are well known.

The Khmer Empire Constructed during the Old Kingdom, the Great Pyramids of Giza serve as enduring representations of human creativity. Built as pharaohs' tombs, these enormous constructions are feats of architecture that display deft alignment and exquisite craftsmanship. Religion and Mythology: With gods like Ra, Isis, and Osiris, Egyptian religious beliefs were fundamental to their civilization. They followed complex funeral customs, temples, and ceremonies as part of their polytheistic religion.

The significance of the afterlife in Egyptian culture is demonstrated by the Book of the Dead, a guide to the hereafter.

Egypt's history was characterized by a number of dynasties and important pharaohs, such as Akhenaten, Thutmose III, Tutankhamun, and Ramses II. These monarchs made significant contributions to the country's architectural legacy, conquests, and religious reforms.

Arts and Sciences: The fields of art, literature, mathematics, and medicine were all flourishing in ancient Egypt. Ancient papyri, the Rosetta Stone, and hieroglyphic writing have all contributed priceless insights into their knowledge and accomplishments.

The Nile River: Known as the "lifeblood of Egypt," the Nile was essential to the country's agriculture and culture. Fertile silt was deposited by the Nile's yearly floods, allowing for abundant harvests and population support.

Decline and Invasion: Greeks, Romans, and Persians all invaded and conquered Egypt, bringing their own cultural influences with them. The Pharaonic era came to an end with the historic association of the final Pharaoh, Cleopatra, with the Romans.

Egypt's history is still developing, and its current state is still influenced by its past. Beyond its pyramids and papyri, ancient Egypt has left a lasting legacy that has influenced global perspectives on civilization, religion, and culture. It continues to stand as a tribute to human effort and history's eternal force.

Chapter 3 : Accommodations

Egypt's lodging options are diverse and can accommodate a wide range of tastes and budgets, so any visitor can find a comfortable place to stay while they explore this fascinating nation.

1. Luxurious Hotels: Cairo and the Red Sea coast are home to a large number of Egypt's opulent hotels. These five-star establishments have lavish accommodations, fine cuisine, spa services, and breathtaking vistas. They frequently have private beaches, swimming areas, and first-rate service.

2. Mid-Range Hotels: There are several mid-range hotels available for tourists looking to strike a balance between comfort and cost. These establishments are well-suited for touring Egypt's highlights since they have cozy accommodations, respectable facilities, and handy locations.

3. Low-Cost Accommodations: Particularly in well-known tourist locations, travelers on a tight budget can choose from a range of hostels, guesthouses, and reasonably priced hotels. Despite having modest amenities, these choices offer an affordable way to see Egypt.

4. Boutique & Unique Stays: Characteristic and unique boutique hotels and guesthouses can be found throughout Egypt. A rich cultural experience is offered by the historic structures that house some of these properties.

5. Resorts: A plethora of beachfront resorts appeal to sun worshippers and lovers of water sports around the Red Sea and other beach areas.

These resorts frequently provide a variety of activities in addition to all-inclusive packages.

6. Nile Cruises: Traveling through Egypt on a Nile boat offers an experience unlike any other. These trips offer a unique way to explore the marvels of the Nile and range from opulent to rustic felucca boats.

Egypt's lodging options suit a wide range of budgets and travel preferences, so you can unwind in comfort and take in the amazing history, culture, and scenic beauty of the nation.

Hotels And Resorts Egypt's

Egypt has a wide variety of hotels and resorts to suit different tastes and price ranges, ranging from opulent beachfront resorts to hotels in historic cities. An overview of the different kinds of lodging available in Egypt is provided below:

1. Luxurious Hotels: Cairo and the Red Sea coast are home to many of Egypt's top-notch luxury hotels. These five-star establishments include luxurious accommodations, first-rate dining options, flawless service, and amazing extras. The Ritz-Carlton, Oberoi, and Four Seasons are a few well-known choices.

2. Mid-Range Hotels: You may find a lot of mid-range hotels in well-known travel locations including Aswan, Luxor, and Cairo. They are the perfect choice for budget-conscious guests seeking luxurious accommodations with contemporary conveniences and cozy rooms.

3. Low-Cost Accommodations: There are several inexpensive hotels, guesthouses, and hostels in Egypt for tourists on a tight budget.

These choices provide straightforward accommodations, minimal facilities, and an affordable way to see the nation's sights.

4. Beach Resorts: Egypt has a large number of beach resorts along its Red Sea coast. The seaside resorts in places like Sharm el-Sheikh and Hurghada are well-known for providing a variety of activities, water sports, and all-inclusive packages.

5. Nile Cruises: Traveling across Egypt on a Nile cruise provides a distinctive lodging experience. Cruises offer a unique approach to see historical places along the Nile; they range from ancient felucca boats to opulent ships.

6. Historic Boutique Hotels: You can find boutique hotels that offer a distinctive and culturally absorbing stay in places like Luxor and Cairo. These hotels are frequently built in historic buildings.

Egypt has a wide variety of hotel alternatives, so visitors can choose the kind of lodging that best fits their needs, be it luxury, a taste of the local way of life, beachside relaxation, or an affordable place to stay while they explore this amazing country.

Traditional Egyptian Accommodation

Experience the culture and history of Egypt in a genuine and immersing way by staying in traditional accommodations. These accommodations, which are frequently located in historic districts, give guests a distinctive window into the past while yet providing for their comfort. Here are few instances:

1. Riads: riads are historic guest houses or boutique hotels found in places like Luxor and Cairo.

These frequently include center courtyards with elaborate tilework, lush gardens, and a peaceful ambience. You may enjoy classic Egyptian architecture and decor when you stay in a riad.

2. Nubian Houses: You may see Nubian houses along the Nile River in places like Aswan, some of which have been converted into lodging for visitors. These vibrant, domed buildings are a reflection of Nubian culture and provide a delightful, culturally immersive stay.

3. Desert Camps: Authentic desert camps offer a distinctive experience for those exploring Egypt's vast deserts. Typically, these are tents in the Bedouin style with rudimentary facilities. You may connect with the desert's natural beauty and the area's nomadic past by staying in a desert tent.

4. Houseboats: Houseboats are a distinctive way to experience Egyptian hospitality around the Nile and other waterways.

These floating lodgings provide a tranquil environment, views of the riverbanks, and an opportunity to observe life as it happens by the water.

In addition to offering a genuine experience, lodging in traditional Egyptian style also helps to support the local community and protect cultural heritage.

It's a great way to take in the customs and history of the nation while experiencing the friendly welcome of the locals. alternatives to fit varying budgets.

Options For Different Budgets

Egypt is a place that can accommodate vacationers of all budgets, as it offers a wide range of possibilities.

1. Low-Cost Travel:

• Hostels: Egypt offers a variety of affordable hostels, especially in the country's main cities and popular tourist locations. These provide private rooms and dorm- style accommodations at incredibly low prices.

• Guesthouses: Conventional guesthouses, which are frequently housed in ancient buildings, offer modest yet comfortable lodging. They are a great option for tourists on a tight budget who want to have real experiences.

• Street Food: Having a taste of Egypt's cuisine may be both tasty and reasonably priced. Street food sellers sell affordable regional fare such as falafel, shawarma, and koshari.

2. Mid-Range Travel:

• 3-Star Hotels: Mid-range hotels are widely available and offer cozy accommodations with contemporary conveniences. For travelers looking for a good mix of comfort and price, they are a fantastic choice.

• Nile Cruises: Comfort and affordability are combined in mid-range Nile cruises. Discover the historical landmarks of Egypt while lounging comfortably in your aboard accommodations.

3. Luxurious Travel:

• 5-Star Hotels: Egypt has opulent 5-star hotels located in its resort areas and main cities. These have luxurious accommodations, excellent food, and first-rate facilities.

- Luxurious Nile Cruises: If you're looking for a lavish experience, luxury Nile cruises are an option.

These provide opulent lodgings, fine dining, and individualized attention while touring historical locations.

Red Sea Vacations: Travelers seeking an upscale beach vacation might find themselves catered to by opulent beachfront resorts along the Red Sea coast. These properties provide top-notch amenities, water activities, and unique experiences.

Egypt offers a wide variety of lodging and dining alternatives to suit all budgets, so visitors can take in the history, culture, and scenic beauty of the nation without worrying about breaking the bank.

Chapter 4:
Eating And Cooking

Egyptian food is a delectable fusion of flavors, shaped by the country's rich history and cultural variety. Eating is a lovely experience in Egypt, where a wide variety of dishes will entice your palate. Introducing you to Egypt's gastronomic world:

1. Traditional Dishes:

- Koshari: A well-liked street food dish consisting of rice, lentils, macaroni, and chickpeas, garnished with tomato sauce and crispy fried onions.
- Falafel: Pita bread is typically accompanied by tahini sauce, veggies, and deep-fried balls made from ground chickpeas or fava beans.

● Molokhia: Served with rice and either chicken or rabbit, this green soup is made from the leaves of the Egyptian mallow plant.

Ta'ameya: A fava bean-based dish that is similar to falafel and is seasoned with herbs.

2. Meat Dishes:

● Kebabs: Grilled meats, like chicken or lamb, that are typically topped with tahini and pita bread.

● Mansaf: A classic Jordanian meal that is well-liked in Egypt, consisting of lamb cooked in dried yogurt that has been fermented and eaten with rice.

3. Seafood:

Egypt provides a wide variety of fresh seafood, such as grilled fish, shrimp, and calamari, thanks to its extensive coastline that stretches along the Mediterranean and Red Seas.

4. Desserts and Sweets:

- Baklava: Phyllo pastry layers stuffed with nuts and enhanced with honey or syrup.
- Kunafa: A sweet syrup-soaked thin pastry that resembles noodles.
- Basbousa: An almond-topped semolina cake drenched in rose or orange blossom water.

5. Drinks:

- Hibiscus Tea (Karkadeh): A revitalizing red tea prepared from dried hibiscus blossoms.
- Mint Tea: A well-liked herbal tea that's typically served hot and sweetened.

6. Street Food: Egypt has a thriving street food culture with a wide range of dishes like roasted sweet potatoes, grilled corn, and ful medames (fava bean stew).

7. Culture of Dining:

- Egyptians eat together with their loved ones on a regular basis, and mealtime is a social occasion. Eating with your right hand is customary, as is saying "bon appétit" to individuals seated next to you.

Egyptian food offers a varied culinary landscape that represents the history and culture of the nation. It is a fusion of traditional recipes and contemporary influences. Egyptian food is certain to make an impression on your taste buds whether you're enjoying a classic restaurant meal or a simple street food snack.

Egyptian Food And Culinary Traditions

Egyptian cuisine and cooking customs include a wide variety of ingredients, flavors from antiquity, and regional influences. Egypt's food is as varied as its scenery, and it is a reflection of the nation's cultural past.

Essential Components:

1. Stable ingredients:

• Bread (Aish): In Egypt, bread is a must-have for every meal. The round, flatbread known as aish baladi is especially well-liked.

• Rice: Rice is used in many different dishes and is typically served as a side dish.

• Legumes: Fava beans and lentils are frequently utilized, particularly in meals such as ful medite.

• Fresh Vegetables: A variety of greens, tomatoes, cucumbers, and eggplants are frequently used in salads, stews, and side dishes.

2. Spices & Seasonings:

• Onions, Garlic, and Herbs: These provide depth of flavor and serve as the foundation for many Egyptian meals.

• Coriander and cumin: These spices are frequently used to season vegetables and meats.

- Mint, parsley, and dill: A lot of fresh herbs are used to give meals a cool touch.

3. Often Caught Dishes:

- Koshari: A well-liked Egyptian meal that consists of rice, spaghetti, lentils, chickpeas, and fried onions that are crispy and served with a hot tomato sauce.
- Molokhia: Traditionally eaten with rice and meat, this green soup is made from the leaves of the Egyptian mallow plant.
- Mahshi: Rice, herbs, and sometimes minced meat are filled into vegetables such as eggplants, zucchinis, and grape leaves.
- Shawarma: Roasted and marinated meat, typically accompanied by veggies and tahini on pita bread.
- Mezze: A selection of tiny appetizers such as falafel, baba ganoush, and hummus.

4. Desserts & Sweets:

- Baklava: Nut-filled layers of phyllo pastry sweetened with syrup.
- Kunafa: A sweet syrup-soaked thin pastry that resembles noodles.
- Basbousa: An almond-topped semolina cake drenched in rose or orange blossom water.

5. Tea and Drinks: • Hibiscus Tea (Karkadeh): Dried hibiscus blossoms are used to make this well-liked, crimson-colored tea. It is pleasant.
- Mint Tea: A calming infusion of herbs, usually served hot and sweetened.

With distinctive variations, Egypt's culinary legacy exhibits the influences of Greek, Turkish, Persian, and Middle Eastern cuisines. Egyptian food offers a delectable and engaging cultural experience, taking travelers on a pleasant culinary tour through the history, customs, and flavors of the nation.

Must-Try Dishes And Local Restaurants

There are a plethora of meals that you simply must sample when traveling Egypt, showcasing the nation's diverse culinary traditions. Here are a few famous foods and the nearby eateries where you may enjoy them:

1. Koshari: A delicious combination of rice, lentils, macaroni, chickpeas, and fried onions, topped with a fiery tomato sauce, this meal is a staple of Egyptian cuisine. Visit the storied restaurant "Abou Tarek" in Cairo, which is well-known for this dish, for a genuine Koshari experience.

2. Magdalena Ful: Ful medames, a wholesome and filling breakfast favorite, is made with slow-cooked fava beans seasoned with olive oil, garlic, and lemon. Cairo's "Felfela" is well known for its delectable ful medames.

Hawawshi #

3: Hawaiiwshi: is a savory Egyptian sandwich made with minced meat (typically lamb or beef) combined with spices and herbs and baked in flatbread. Cairo's "El Abd" has some of the best hawawshi around.

4. Molokhia: Traditionally served with rice and your choice of meat (typically chicken or rabbit), this green soup is created from the leaves of the Egyptian mallow plant. To experience real molokhia, go to "Sobhy Kaber" in Cairo.

5. Ta'ameya: A popular street dish, ta'ameya is similar to falafel but cooked with fava beans and seasonings. In Cairo, "Mahmoud's Ta'ameya" is well-known for its mouthwatering and crispy ta'ameya sandwiches.

6. Mahshi: Egyptians love their stuffed veggies. Examples of these include mahshi wara'enab, which is filled with grape leaves, and mahshi kousa, which is stuffed zucchini. In Cairo, try "Feteera Cafe" for some delicious takes on these recipes.

7. Umm Ali: Umm ali is a traditional Egyptian delicacy consisting of a creamy bread pudding stuffed with raisins, almonds, and coconut. "Umm Ali Café" is a popular location in Cairo to savor this delicious treat.

8. Roz Bel Laban: A popular Egyptian dish, this rice pudding is created with creamy, sweetened milk and perfumed with rose or vanilla extract. Try it in Cairo at the "Naguib Mahfouz Cafe".

9. Grilled Seafood: You must take advantage of the chance to have freshly grilled fish, shrimp, and calamari throughout the Mediterranean and Red Sea shores. In Sharm el-Sheikh, eateries such as "Fish Market" provide a delightful seafood experience.

Diverse palates can be satisfied by the abundance of tastes and cuisines found in Egyptian cuisine. Discovering neighborhood restaurants and street food vendors is a fun way to sample regional cuisine and become fully immersed in Egypt's culinary culture.

Dietary Considerations

It's crucial to know about dietary restrictions before traveling to Egypt in order to have a relaxing and comfortable stay. The following are important things to remember:

1. Halal cuisine: Since the majority of Egyptians are Muslims, halal cuisine is served at most restaurants and food establishments. Pork is rarely found on menus because it is not eaten in Islamic diets.

2. Vegetarian and Vegan Options: A variety of vegetarian and vegan cuisines are available in Egypt. You can savor meatless meals like falafel, vegetarian koshari, ful medames, and an assortment of mezze (small plates).

3. Allergies and Dietary Restrictions: When dining out, it's critical to express your needs clearly if you have any dietary restrictions or food allergies. It's advisable to do your homework and make plans in advance to find appropriate selections, even though certain restaurants may fulfill customized demands.

4. Hydration: Egypt's weather can be hot and dry, so it's important to drink plenty of water. To avoid contracting a waterborne infection, drink bottled water and make sure all fruits and vegetables are cleaned or peeled.

5. Street Food: There are many delectable options available for street food, which is highly popular. To prevent any health hazards, it is best to proceed with caution when eating street cuisine. Seek out occupied sellers who maintain proper cleanliness.

6. Herbs and Spices: A wide range of herbs and spices are used in Egyptian cooking. You can ask for foods to be served softer or without specific seasonings if you have a sensitivity to certain spices or specific tastes.

7. Ramadan: Be advised that many eateries may have restricted hours or be closed throughout the day if you happen to visit during the holy month of Ramadan. During the hours of fasting, it is considerate to abstain from eating, drinking, or smoking in public.

8. Tipping: In Egypt, especially in the service sector, leaving a gratuity is common. Having small amounts of Egyptian Pounds (EGP) on hand is a good idea when tipping restaurant employees.

You may fully appreciate Egypt's varied and savory food options while honoring local customs and making the most of your trip experience by taking these dietary considerations into account and being open to experiencing local cuisine.

Chapter 5 :

Exploring Egypts Heritage

Discovering Egypt's rich history is like taking a trip through thousands of years of history, with a fascinating tapestry of historical wonders and cultural riches. The following are some of the most important facets of Egyptian history that tourists can discover:

1. Ancient Monuments: Egypt is home to renowned historical sites including the Sphinx, the Luxor and Karnak temples, and the Giza Pyramids. These works of architecture are magnificent examples of ancient Egyptian civilization.

2. Valley of the Kings: Pharaohs were buried in rock-cut tombs at this necropolis on the west bank of the Nile close to Luxor. Explore these ornate chambers to view complex hieroglyphs and prehistoric artwork.

3. Egyptian Museum: This Cairo-based museum is home to a vast array of items, including mummies, innumerable relics from ancient Egypt, and the riches of Tutankhamun.

4. Islamic and Coptic legacy: The Islamic and Coptic Christian influences are part of Egypt's cultural legacy. Discover ancient Coptic landmarks like the Hanging Church in Cairo and mosques like Al-Azhar Mosque.

5. Nubian Culture: Travelers can learn about the Nubian people's heritage, which includes their distinctive language, art, and customs, by visiting Aswan.

6. Desert Treks: Ancient trade routes, rock art, and archeological sites can be found all over Egypt's deserts. Discovering the Western Desert and the oasis of Bahariya and Siwa is a historical and scenic journey.

7. ancient Crafts: Egypt's ancient crafts, such as its elaborate carpet weaving, ceramics, and papyrus art, are another way that the country's legacy is kept alive. You may see and buy these handcrafted handicrafts in neighborhood markets and workshops.

8. Nile Cruises: With stops at numerous historical sites and insights into Egypt's ancient and present cultures, cruising along the Nile River lets visitors fully immerse themselves in the country's legacy.

Discovering Egypt's legacy is a journey through the annals of human civilization, allowing tourists to see the long-lasting effects of a country that has influenced art, culture, and history for countless years. This trip offers a deep comprehension of our common history.

Pyramids, Temples, And Ancient Sites In Egypt

The amazing accomplishments of one of the oldest and most resilient civilizations in history are demonstrated by the pyramids, temples, and other ancient sites found in Egypt. These historical sites continue to draw tourists from all over the world and offer a glimpse into the splendor of ancient Egypt.

1. The Giza Pyramids: The Great Pyramid and other Pyramids of Giza are well-known representations of ancient Egypt. They were constructed as pharaohs' tombs and have stood for more than 4,500 years. Built for Pharaoh Khufu, the Great Pyramid is still regarded as one of the Seven Wonders of the Ancient World.

2. Sphinx: The massive statue known as the Sphinx, which has the head of a pharaoh and the body of a lion, guards the Giza Plateau.

3. Luxor and Karnak Temples: The Luxor Temple and the Karnak Temple complex are located in Luxor, which was formerly the ancient city of Thebes. The Sphinx is thought to symbolize Pharaoh Khafre and is closely connected to the pyramids. These temples, which have enormous columns, statues, and hieroglyphics decorating them, are devoted to a variety of gods and pharaohs.

4. Valley of the Kings: The Valley of the Kings is a burial place for New Kingdom pharaohs and is situated in Luxor on the west bank of the Nile. Tutankhamun's tomb is among the many ornately decorated ones housed within.

5. Abu Simbel: Among Egypt's most magnificent structures are the temples of Abu

Simbel. Constructed by Ramses II, these enormous monuments with their elaborate sculptures were moved to a higher location to keep them from being submerged by the Nile River.

6. The temples at Edfu and Kom Ombo: These temples beside the Nile are devoted to the gods Sobek and Horus, respectively. The reliefs in Edfu Temple are beautifully preserved, while Kom Ombo has a distinctive "double" design.

7. Philae Temple: This temple honors the goddess Isis and is built on an island in the Nile. It was moved to provide a beautiful location when the Aswan High Dam was being built.

8. Saqqara: Often referred to as the "Step Pyramid," the Pyramid of Djoser is one of the oldest pyramids and represents a significant advancement in pyramid design.

These historic landmarks provide light on Egypt's accomplishments throughout history and highlight the importance of a civilization whose cultural, religious, and architectural legacies will never fade. Discovering these riches is a trip through time that provides a strong link to the common history of humanity.

Museums And Historical Landmarks In Egypt

Egypt offers a fascinating tour through its rich history and culture through its many museums and historical sites. The following are a few of Egypt's most renowned historical sites and museums:

1. Cairo's Egyptian Museum: The Egyptian Museum, which is housed in Cairo, is a veritable gold mine of artifacts that depict ancient Egyptian history. It is home to a vast collection that includes sculptures, mummies, innumerable antiquities, and the riches of Tutankhamun.

2. Giza Plateau: The Great Pyramid, the Pyramid of Khafre, and the Pyramid of Menkaure are located on the Giza Plateau, which is an area outside of Cairo.

The Sphinx is a mysterious statue that has the head of a pharaoh and the body of a lion standing next to the pyramids.

3. Luxor's Valley of the Kings: The Valley of the Kings is an old cemetery where the

pharaohs of the New Kingdom were buried. It is home to elaborate tombs with exquisitely preserved hieroglyphic and artistic art, one of which is that of Tutankhamun.

4. The Karnak Temple Complex in Luxor: Dedicated to the god Amun, the Karnak Temple

Complex is a sizable religious complex. It displays an amazing assortment of statues, columns, obelisks, and temples that showcase the magnificence of ancient Egyptian architecture.

5. Luxor Temple: Another amazing historical site is the Luxor Temple, which is situated on the east bank of the Nile. It has imposing statues, intricate carvings, and an avenue of sphinxes and was constructed as a temple for the god Amun.

6. Abu Simbel Temples: Originally built by Ramses II, the Abu Simbel temples were moved to a higher location to protect them from Lake Nasser's increasing waters. These enormous constructions, which showcase the engineering prowess of ancient Egypt, are decorated with elaborate sculptures.

7. Philae Temple: This temple honors the goddess Isis and is located on Philae Island. It was moved to provide a beautiful location among the waters of the Nile as a result of the construction of the Aswan High Dam.

8. Saqqara: The Step Pyramid of Djoser, one of the oldest pyramids in Egypt, is situated in Saqqara, which is close to Cairo. It represents a significant advancement in pyramid design. Discovering these historical sites and museums is like taking a trip through time; it gives one

a deep appreciation of Egypt's rich cultural legacy and the lasting influence of one of the oldest civilizations in history. These locations are important not only for Egypt but also for the global understanding of human civilization and history.

Historical Tours And Archaeological Adventurers

Travelers can explore magnificent archaeological sites and dig into Egypt's rich past with historical tours and archaeological excursions. Uncovering the mysteries of ancient civilizations is one of the many opportunities these trips provide. A sample of the experiences these tours offer is as follows:

1. Pyramids and Sphinx Exploration: The famous Pyramids of Giza and the Sphinx are frequently the first stops on a historical tour of Egypt. Entering the pyramids allows visitors to explore the elaborate rooms and hieroglyphs within, all the while admiring the remarkable architectural achievements of the ancient Egyptians.

2. Valley of the Kings Excursions: A fascinating archeological excursion is discovering Luxor's Valley of the Kings. Entrance to exquisitely adorned tombs, such as the one belonging to Tutankhamun, allows visitors to view the exquisitely preserved artwork and inscriptions.

3. Tours of the Luxor and Karnak Temple Complexes: Travelers on historical tours frequently visit the Luxor and Karnak Temple complexes. These temples, which are replete with enormous statues, obelisks, and avenues of sphinxes, display the magnificence of ancient religious architecture.

4. Abu Simbel Expedition: Tourists can go on an archaeological excursion to Abu Simbel, which is the location of the enormous temples built by Ramses II. By moving these temples to higher ground, we can see the amazing engineering feats of both the ancient and modern eras.

5. Nile Cruises: A lot of historical excursions include Nile River cruises, which let visitors see historical locations by the banks of the river. These cruises provide guests a greater grasp of Egypt's past by frequently stopping at lesser-known archeological sites.

6. Saqqara and Step Pyramid Discovery: The Step Pyramid of Djoser, an early example of a pyramid and an important archaeological monument, is revealed during a tour to Saqqara, which is located close to Cairo.

7. Exploring Dendera and Abydos: Historical excursions may include stops in Dendera and Abydos, where visitors can view the exquisitely preserved temples dedicated to numerous Egyptian deities.

8. Off-road Journeys: Archaeologists who are daring enough can discover lesser-known archeological sites, rock art, and ancient trade networks by venturing into Egypt's deserts. Travelers have unrivaled access to Egypt's ancient sites and archaeological excursions thanks to its historical tours and adventures. From the majesty of the pyramids to the intricate details of temples and tombs, these encounters provide a deeper link to the nation's legacy, making Egypt an incredible destination for both history buffs and adventurers.

Exploring Urban Life And Modern Culture

Discovering Egypt's contemporary culture and urban life provides a striking contrast to its historic ancient landmarks. Here's a peek at Egypt's dynamic urban culture:

1. Cairo: The Bustling Metropolis: Cairo, the capital of Egypt, is a vibrant city that skillfully combines the old and the new. The city is a patchwork of the old and the new, with contemporary buildings contrasting with traditional communities.

Downtown Cairo is home to chic boutiques, galleries of modern art, and a thriving cafe scene. In addition, visitors can explore communities with a reputation for cultural institutions and tree-lined streets, such as Garden City and Zamalek.

2. Arts and Culture: Galleries featuring the creations of gifted regional artists are a feature of Egypt's flourishing modern art scene. A window into the nation's artistic revival is offered by the performances, concerts, and exhibitions held at the Cairo Opera House. A cultural hub, the El Sawy Culturewheel presents a range of events, including movie screenings and musical performances.

3. Food & Dining: Egypt's urban lifestyle provides a wide range of culinary experiences. Cairo's restaurants provide a variety of foreign and Egyptian cuisine, ranging from fine dining to street food.

Dine al fresco at a rooftop restaurant with a view of the Nile or buy street sellers' renditions of traditional Egyptian dishes like ta'amiya and koshari.

4. Shopping and souvenirs: Contemporary shopping districts and thriving markets may be found in Egyptian cities. Cairo's Khan el-Khalili market is well-known for its winding pathways brimming with goods ranging from jewelry and crafts to spices. Additionally, consumers looking for luxury brands are served by boutiques and upmarket shopping centers.

5. Entertainment and Nightlife: Egypt's cities come to life at night. Cairo's nightlife consists of vibrant cafes, clubs, and pubs where you may dance to international and local sounds, see live music, and have shisha with friends.

6. Innovation and Technology: Egypt is leading the way in these areas. Tech firms are based in Cairo's Smart Village, a contemporary business park. The city promotes a developing entrepreneurial culture by holding tech and innovation events.

7. Sports and Fitness: With the availability of gyms, fitness centers, and athletic facilities, Egyptians living in urban areas are becoming more health-conscious. Football and other traditional sports like taekwondo are quite popular; in places like Cairo and Alexandria, you can even watch a football game.

Discovering Egypt's contemporary culture and urban life is an intriguing addition to its historical legacy. It's a chance to see how a nation that strikes a balance between the vitality of modern life and its long-lasting historical history is changing, diverse, and vibrant.

Shopping And Entertainment

Egypt has a thriving entertainment and shopping sector that successfully combines modern and traditional elements.

Here's a peek at everything Egypt has to offer, from vibrant bazaars to modern malls and a variety of entertainment options:

Purchasing:

1. **Cairo's famous Khan el-Khalili :** Khan el-Khalili market is a hive of narrow lanes crammed with stores offering everything from traditional crafts and antiques to jewelry, spices, and textiles. It's the perfect spot to bargain and discover one-of-a-kind trinkets.

2. **Contemporary Malls:** Cairo, Alexandria, and Sharm El Sheikh are just a few of the major Egyptian cities that have contemporary malls. Shopping venues like City Stars Mall and Mall of Arabia are well-liked because they provide a large selection of both local and international brands.

3. **The Souks in Luxor:** These vibrant marketplaces provide a variety of goods, including Egyptian spices, handicrafts, and mementos. It's a terrific location to find

one-of-a-kind things while touring this ancient city.

4. Aswan Craft Market: The market in Aswan is well-known for its Nubian handicrafts, which include vibrant fabrics, jewelry, and ceramics. It's a fantastic place to purchase genuine Nubian mementos.

5. Spice Markets: Spice markets provide a sensual experience all around Egypt. You may buy traditional foods, herbs, and aromatic spices to replicate Egyptian flavors at home.

For entertainment :

1. Theaters & Cinemas: Egypt boasts a thriving theater and film industry. Cinemas screen a variety of foreign and local films, and the Cairo Opera House hosts cultural events.

Known as "Arabic Hollywood," Egyptian cinema releases a large number of films annually.

2. Nightlife: There is a vibrant nightlife scene in major cities like Sharm El Sheikh, Cairo, and Alexandria. You may enjoy a variety of entertainment alternatives and dance the night away in cafes, bars, and nightclubs.

3. Music: Egypt's musical history is extensive. At several locations, you may see live performances of fusion, modern pop, and traditional Arabic music. The "oud," also known as the Arabic lute, is a common instrument used in Egyptian music.

4. Festivals: Egypt holds a number of annual festivals honoring literature, culture, and everything from music and film to film and literature. A few examples are the Sharm El Sheikh International Theater Festival, the Luxor African Film Festival, and the Cairo International Film Festival.

5. Waterfront Promenades: Coastal towns with gorgeous waterfront promenades, such as Alexandria and Sharm El Sheikh, provide lovely places to walk, eat, and take in the picturesque vistas of the Red Sea or Mediterranean.

From visiting ancient bazaars to taking in contemporary entertainment and cultural festivals, Egypt's shopping and entertainment industry provides a wide range of activities. Egypt offers something for everyone, whether your interests are in modern fashion, traditional souvenirs, or deeply engaging cultural experiences.

Chapter 6 :

Nile River Cruises

Egypt's Nile River cruises provide a genuinely enchanted voyage into the center of this historic country.

With a unique perspective on Egypt's history and culture, these cruises sail on the life-giving waters of the Nile. An overview of what makes Nile River cruises unique can be found here:

1. Historical Exploration: Famous locations such as Edfu Temple, Luxor, the Valley of the Kings, and Karnak Temple are frequently visited by cruise ships. Travelers can follow in the footsteps of pharaohs as they tour the ruins of ancient Egypt.

2. Comfort and Luxuriance: Nile cruises provide luxurious cabins, fine meals, and first-rate service. Contemporary ships offer a haven of comfort where visitors can unwind following days of sightseeing.

3. Scenic Beauty: As the trip travels, guests are shown a variety of ever-changing scenery, including verdant riverbanks, views of the desert, and traditional towns. The Nile's sunsets are spectacular.

4. Cultural Immersion: Traditional music and dance performances offer passengers a taste of Egyptian culture, while onboard Egyptologists offer insights into the history of the nation.

5. The Little-Known Treasures of the Nile: Cruises may take you to less-frequented locations, offering a more upscale experience. One special experience is visiting Kom Ombo Temple, which honors the crocodile god Sobek.

6. Relaxation: Cruises provide passengers the chance to lounge on sundecks, swim in the pool, or just observe life as it passes by along the Nile. Cruises down the Nile River provide the ideal fusion of luxury, culture, history, and leisure. These cruises offer an amazing way to see Egypt's enduring legacy, whether your goal is to explore historic temples or just enjoy the splendor of the Nile.

Experiencing The Nile River

Traveling along the serene banks of the Nile River is like setting off on a timeless adventure through the center of Egypt, where culture and history collide. This mythical river, known as the "lifeblood of Egypt," has a particular place in the hearts of Egyptians and provides an exciting and one-of-a-kind experience.

Sail Along the Nile: The finest way to experience a trip down the Nile is on a contemporary cruise ship or a classic felucca. The journey starts with soft breezes filling the sails or with the opulent amenities of a cruise ship.

You'll be enthralled with the constantly shifting landscape of lush farmland, charming villages, and banks dotted with palm trees as you flow down the river.

Discovering Ancient Wonders: Historical artifacts litter the banks of the Nile. Ancient Egypt's open-air museums, Luxor and Karnak, tell their history with the help of enormous sculptures, complex hieroglyphs, and the remains of temples. Pharaohs' resting place, the Valley of the Kings, has elaborate tombs that hide mysteries.

Experiencing Local Life: Traveling down the Nile provides a window into Egyptian daily life. You'll visit Nubian communities where the residents warmly greet you and discuss their customs. One amazing aspect of the trip is the contrast between the tranquil beauty of the river and the daily bustling.

Nile Sunsets and Starry Skies: The serene waters of the Nile make for an ideal setting for breathtaking sunsets and, on clear nights, a starry sky. Sip mint tea or Egyptian coffee on your veranda while watching the sky change hues and the river mirroring the region's ancient history.

A trip along the Nile River transports you back in time and culture. This trip is one of the most remarkable experiences Egypt has to offer since it blends the classic charm of antiquity with the contemporary conveniences of cruising.

Cruise Options And Itineraries In Egypt

Egypt lets visitors experience its rich history, gorgeous scenery, and lively culture through a variety of enthralling cruise options along the Red Sea and the Nile. These are a few well-liked cruise choices and itineraries:

1. Nile River Cruises:

- Luxury Nile Cruises: These cruises provide the highest level of accommodation, along with roomy cabins, fine cuisine, and knowledgeable guides who show you around famous locations. A typical schedule can include stops at historic villages, temples, and tombs along the way, as well as trips to Luxor and Aswan.

- Felucca Sailing: Take a trip aboard an authentic Egyptian sailboat, or felucca, for a more traditional experience. These cruises offer a laid-back travel experience with basic lodging, giving guests a fresh take on the allure of the Nile.

• Dahabiya Cruises: Usually consisting of a small number of staterooms, these boutique cruises offer a cozy atmosphere. You'll discover lesser-known locations, delight in individualized attention, and take in the calm environment.

2. Red Sea Cruises:

• Red Sea Liveaboard Diving: Take a liveaboard tour to discover the stunning underwater environment of the Red Sea. Egypt is a diver's paradise with its immaculate coral reefs, abundant marine life, and well-known dive spots like Ras Mohammed and the Brothers Islands.

• Leisure Cruises: The Red Sea coast provides leisure cruises where you may visit coastal towns like Hurghada and Sharm el-Sheikh, which are renowned for their stunning beaches and exciting nightlife, and unwind on deck while participating in water sports.

3. Cruises in Lake Nasser:

• Lake Nasser Cruises: These boats take you to Lake Nasser, which was formed when the Aswan High Dam was built.

It is a beautiful lake. You will explore the secluded splendor of the lake's environs and see temples that have been moved to higher land, such as Abu Simbel.

Egypt cruise itineraries cover a wide range of interests, from Red Sea underwater research to historical travel along the Nile. Egypt's cruise options guarantee amazing experiences amidst the country's ageless allure, whether you prefer luxury, tradition, or adventure.

Exploring Egypt Coastline Beauty

Discovering Egypt's stunning coastline offers a lovely trip along the coasts of the Mediterranean and Red Sea, along with a variety of landscapes, water sports, and cultural experiences. Here's a peek at what draws people to Egypt's coastal regions:

Mediterranean coast :

- Alexandria: Alexandria, dubbed the "Pearl of the Mediterranean," offers a singular fusion of culture, history, and waterfront splendor. Explore the historic Bibliotheca Alexandrina, stroll down the Corniche, and unwind on the stunning beaches of the city.

Marsa Matrouh: This seaside city is well-known for its gorgeous sandy beaches and glistening clean waters. It's the perfect place to sunbathe, go snorkeling, and swim.

2. Red Sea Coast:

- Sharm El Sheikh: Renowned as a diving and snorkeling destination worldwide, Sharm El Sheikh is situated at the southernmost point of the Sinai Peninsula. Underwater adventures in the Red Sea are captivating due to their vivid coral reefs.

- Hurghada: Well-known for its water activities, such as windsurfing, kiteboarding, and parasailing, Hurghada is another well-liked Red Sea resort. It also provides chances to visit other islands like Mahmya and Giftun.

- Marsa Alam: For those looking for a quiet beach getaway, this sleepy village is ideal.

Marsa Alam is a great place to dive and snorkel because of its pristine coral reefs and abundant marine life.

3. Coastal Activities:

- Boat rides, jet skiing, snorkeling, and scuba diving are just a few of the water sports available along Egypt's coast. The Red Sea, in particular, is well-known for its colorful coral reefs and rich marine life.

- Those who prefer water sports can sail, windsurf, and kiteboard in the Red Sea's consistent winds.

4. Relaxation by the Sea:
- Tourists may spend their beach holidays in luxury thanks to the lovely resorts and hotels that line the coastal districts.

- spend beachside dining and spa services while unwinding on sandy beaches and watching breathtaking sunsets over the waters.

Egypt's shoreline is a mesmerizing fusion of contemporary conveniences and natural beauties, providing visitors with a wide variety of experiences. Egypt's Mediterranean and Red Sea shores have a lot to offer, whether you're an adventurer or just seeking a peaceful beach vacation.

Diving And Water Sports :

Divers and lovers of water sports will find paradise on Egypt's Red Sea shoreline. Here's a taste of what water activities this lively area has to offer:

Scuba diving: The Red Sea in Egypt is well known for its scuba diving options. It is one of the best places in the world for diving because of the pristine seas, colorful coral reefs, and abundant marine life. There are sites that are appropriate for divers of all skill levels, regardless of experience level.

Discover underwater caverns, coral gardens, and sunken wrecks while seeing vibrant fish, rays, sharks, and other marine life.

Snorkeling: Snorkeling in the Red Sea is a gratifying activity that offers a more relaxed underwater experience. From the surface, snorkelers may appreciate the magnificence of the coral reefs, and many resorts offer convenient access to snorkeling locations just off the beach.

Kiteboarding and windsurfing: The Red Sea is a windsurfing and kiteboarding haven due to its steady winds. Locations like Hurghada and Dahab provide ideal circumstances for these thrilling water activities. For novices and experienced aficionados both, lessons and equipment rentals are easily accessible.

Sailing: A tranquil way to take in the coastline beauty of the Red Sea is to sail around it. Relaxing and picturesque experiences may be had aboard catamarans and traditional Felucca boats, which can be used for extended sailing expeditions or sunset cruises.

Jet-skiing: Along the coast of the Red Sea, thrill-seekers can indulge their urge for speed by taking up jet-skiing.

For individuals who want to experience the exhilaration of sailing across the ocean, rentals and guided tours are offered.

Egypt's coastal regions provide a variety of aquatic adventures against a backdrop of breathtaking natural beauty, whether you're an experienced diver looking to explore the depths of the Red Sea's spectacular underwater world or a water sports enthusiast seeking wind and waves.

Chapter 7 : Transportation

Travelers can tour Egypt's rich history, cities, and coastal regions with relative ease because of the country's numerous transportation options, which combine modern and ancient ways. An outline of Egypt's transportation choices is provided below:

1. Metro: The metro systems in Cairo and Alexandria provide a practical and reasonably priced way to get about these busy cities. Particularly, the metro in Cairo is among the busiest in the Middle East.

2. Buses: Throughout Egypt, buses are a popular means of transportation that link towns and cities. There are affordable travel choices offered by both public and private bus operators.

3. Trains: Egypt's rail system links the country's main cities and is a great way to see the interior of the nation. Sleeper trains, like the "Sleeper Express," provide cozy overnight travel between Aswan, Luxor, and Cairo.

4. Taxis: In cities, taxis are widely accessible. Before you leave, make sure the taxi has a meter or decide on a fare. Major cities also see high usage of local service providers and ride-hailing applications like Uber.

5. Domestic Flights: Domestic flights are an effective means of long-distance travel within Egypt. Three major hubs for domestic air travel are Cairo International Airport, Hurghada International Airport, and Sharm El Sheikh International Airport.

6. Ferries and Boats: Ferries and boats offer distinctive modes of transit along the Nile River and in coastal areas. Accessing historical monuments and islands can be a delightful experience when traveling by boat.

7. Horse-drawn carriages and camels: These traditional modes of transportation are employed for short trips in several places, including Luxor and Aswan, and they provide a glimpse into the native way of life.

8. Rental Cars: For travelers seeking convenience and flexibility, renting a car is an alternative. It's a fantastic option for travel to beach resorts or for discovering lesser-known locations.

9. Microbuses and Metro: Cairo features a network of microbuses that service neighborhoods and locations that are difficult for larger buses to reach in addition to the metro.

Egypt's varied transportation network makes it easy for visitors to see contemporary cities, stunning coastlines, and archaeological sites.

Even while major cities have well-developed infrastructure, there can be fewer transportation options in rural and isolated places, so it's best to prepare ahead for a hassle-free and pleasurable trip.

Getting To Egypt

Egypt's internationally connected airports and ports make traveling there comparatively easy. Here's a summary of how to get to this fascinating location:

By Air: The main entry point for foreign visitors to Egypt is Cairo International Airport, which is the country's biggest and busiest airport. It welcomes planes arriving from key global cities. Other noteworthy international airports serving visitors to the Red Sea resorts are Hurghada International Airport and Sharm El Sheikh International Airport.

By Sea: Alexandria and Port Said are important ports of entry for passengers arriving by cruise ship. Egypt is frequently included as a stop on cruise ship itineraries, giving travelers the chance to see historical monuments along the Nile and explore coastal cities.

Visa Requirements :

It's crucial to confirm the necessary visa requirements for your country of residence before departing for Egypt.

The majority of visitors can get a 30-day visa upon arrival, although some might need to apply ahead of time. Make sure the validity of your passport is at least six months beyond the date you plan to depart.

Points of Entry:

Cairo International Airport is the busiest entrance point into Egypt, handling the majority of foreign visitors. Both Hurghada and Sharm El

Sheikh International Airports serve as important entrance points for travelers visiting Red Sea destinations. Egypt is a well-liked holiday destination due to its friendly approach toward visitors and rich cultural heritage.

Travel preparations :

It's a good idea to check the current travel advisories, visa requirements, and safety alerts from your home country's government while making travel plans to Egypt. Furthermore, as these may change, confirm the most recent COVID-19 travel guidelines and restrictions.

Domestic Linkages:

Due to Egypt's well-established domestic transportation system, getting to different parts of the nation is simple. Longer distances can be covered by domestic planes, although major cities are connected by the train system.

Additional choices for traveling to different places include buses and cabs.

Final Remarks:

The first step to enjoying Egypt's colorful culture, extensive history, and breathtaking landscapes is getting there. Egypt provides visitors from all over the world with the opportunity to experience its classic marvels and cutting-edge pleasures thanks to its numerous international airports and immaculate ports. Make sure to thoroughly organize your itinerary and keep up with local customs and entry requirements for a trouble-free and enjoyable trip.

Getting Around Within The Country

Traveling throughout Egypt is a rather easy and well-connected experience because of the variety of transportation options available to those who want to explore the historical sites and different landscapes of the nation.

1. Metro: The effective metro systems in Alexandria and Cairo make navigating these congested cities simple. Among the busiest in the Middle East is the Cairo Metro, which links several areas and sites.

2. Buses: Egypt's national bus network links the nation's cities, towns, and provinces. There are both private and public bus services available, offering affordable transit choices. Comfortable seating is a feature of long-distance buses designed for interstate transportation.

3. Trains: Egypt's vast rail network links several important cities, such as Cairo, Alexandria, Luxor, Aswan, and more. Sleeper trains, like the "Sleeper Express," provide a pleasant and cozy means of transportation between cities, particularly on overnight trips.

4. Taxis: In cities, taxis are widely accessible. Prior to beginning the trip, it is advisable to confirm that the taxi has a functional meter or to agree on a fare. In big cities, ride-hailing applications like Uber are also well-liked.

5. Domestic Flights: Domestic flights are quick and convenient for long-distance travel within Egypt. The main hubs for domestic air travel are Cairo International Airport, Hurghada International Airport, and Sharm El Sheikh International Airport.

6. Ferries and Boats: Ferries and boats offer distinctive modes of transit along the Nile River and in coastal areas. These can be an easy and beautiful method to get to historical places, including islands.

7. Horse-drawn carriages and camels: These ancient modes of transportation are still in use in several places, especially Luxor and Aswan, and provide an enlightening cultural experience for short trips.

8. Rental Cars: If you're looking for ease and flexibility when traveling, renting a car can be a good alternative, especially if you want to visit less-traveled locations or coastal resorts.

9. Metro and Microbuses: Cairo features a network of microbuses that service communities and locations that are difficult for larger buses to reach in addition to the metro. These microbuses provide an affordable means of transportation throughout the city.

10. Carpooling: In cities, ride-sharing applications are becoming more and more common since they offer a simple and practical way to schedule transportation.

Travelers may reasonably easily explore Egypt's historical monuments, towns, and coastal regions because of the country's well-developed transportation infrastructure. Because every kind of transportation has its own set of benefits, it's critical to choose your mode of transportation based on your itinerary and the places you want to visit.

Domestic Flights And Ground Transport

Egypt makes it easy for visitors to visit different parts of the country because of its well-connected domestic flight and ground transportation network.

Domestic Travel:

1. Cairo International Airport: With connections to several domestic locations, Cairo International Airport serves as the main entry point. It serves as a hub for tourists going to other Egyptian towns.

2. Sharm El Sheikh International Airport: This airport serves the well-known Red Sea resort town and offers access to the southern Sinai Peninsula, Dahab, and other major tourist destinations.

3. Hurghada International Airport: Situated on the Red Sea coast, Hurghada International Airport serves as a significant hub for tourists visiting Red Sea destinations such El Gouna, Marsa Alam, and Hurghada.

4. Luxor International Airport: With connections to places like Luxor, Aswan, and the temples of Karnak and Luxor, Luxor International Airport is a great place to explore Upper Egypt.

5. Alexandria International Airport: This airport serves travel to Alexandria and neighboring Mediterranean coast locations. It is located in the second-largest city in Egypt.

6. Marsa Alam International Airport: This airport is a practical option for those heading to Marsa Alam and its immaculate beaches.

Ground transportation :

1. Trains: Major cities in Egypt are connected by a vast train network. Longer trips are best served by cozy sleeper trains, which offer a quick and easy way to get between Alexandria, Luxor, Aswan, and Cairo.

2. Buses: Throughout the nation, buses connect cities, towns, and regions on their routes, making them a popular form of ground transportation. There are both private and public bus services available, offering reasonably priced travel choices.

3. Taxis: A convenient means of transportation for exploring cities and their environs, taxis are widely accessible in urban areas. Before the trip starts, it's crucial to confirm if the taxi has a working meter or to agree on a fare.

4. Rental Cars: For visitors looking for freedom and flexibility, renting a car is a practical choice. It's a fantastic option for road excursions to historical sites and coastal resorts, as well as for exploring less-traveled places.

5. Ferries and Boats: Ferries and boats provide distinctive modes of transit along the Nile River and in coastal areas, especially for visiting islands and historical monuments.

6. Microbuses: Microbuses in Cairo offer an inexpensive means of transportation across the city by serving communities and places that are difficult for larger buses to reach.

Domestic flights and Egypt's ground transportation network give visitors the opportunity to discover the nation's rich cultural legacy, amazing ancient sites, vibrant cities, and stunning coastline. The kind of transportation you select will rely on your itinerary and the areas you want to see; each has special benefits for learning about Egypt's history and natural beauty.

Chapter 8 :

Health And Safety

For your trip to Egypt to be fulfilling and worry-free, you must make sure you are safe and in good health. In Egypt, keep the following points in mind for your health and safety:

Security:

1. Individual possessions: Pay attention to your possessions, particularly in busy places and popular tourist destinations. To stop theft, use money belts and secure baggage.

2. Regional Rites: Get acquainted with Egyptian traditions and manners. When attending places of worship, dress modestly and follow local customs.

3. Guided Tours: Take into account guided tours for your safety and to learn about the place, particularly while visiting less-traveled locations.

4. Health Safety Measures: To prevent contracting a foodborne illness, exercise caution when buying food or beverages from street sellers. Refrain from drinking raw or peeled fruits and vegetables and stick to bottled water.

Wellness:

1. vaccines: Find out if any vaccines are necessary or advised before visiting Egypt. Typhoid, hepatitis A, and regular vaccinations are examples of common vaccinations.

2. Travel Insurance: Take into account getting travel insurance that includes coverage for both medical emergencies and trip disruptions or cancellations.

3. Sun Protection: To prevent sunburn, wear protective clothing, sunscreen, and sunglasses in

Egypt because the country's sun is known for its intensity.

4. Hydration: Maintain adequate hydration, particularly in arid areas and during hot weather. Opt for bottled water instead of tap water or ice in your beverages.

5. Medical Facilities: There are contemporary hospitals and medical facilities in large cities like Cairo and Alexandria. For minor medical emergencies, it is important to have a basic medical kit on hand.

6. Prescription Drugs: Make sure you have enough prescription drugs for your trip if you need them. Keep a copy of your prescriptions with you, and find out whether these drugs are available in Egypt.

7. Egyptian Cuisine: Although street food is generally tasty, be cautious when attempting it, particularly if you have a sensitive stomach.

8. Guidelines for COVID-19: Keep yourself informed about any changes to the COVID-19 rules, since they may involve testing and quarantine restrictions. Observe local health regulations.

around prudent safety and health measures, you can maximize your experience traveling around Egypt while lowering your risk. Like any travel destination, the secret to a safe and happy trip is to be well-informed and prepared.

traveler safety tips :

Egypt can be a fascinating and interesting place to visit, but as with any place, safety should always come first. The following travel safety advice may help you have a hassle-free and joyful trip to Egypt:

1. Planning and Research:

- Verify Travel Warnings: Examine the safety instructions and travel advisories that your government's foreign affairs department has provided before your trip. This will update you on Egypt's current state of affairs.

• Travel Insurance: Invest in all-inclusive travel insurance that includes coverage for lost luggage, medical emergencies, and trip cancellations. Make sure you have copies of your policy and your contact details on hand in case you require help.

• Regional Laws and Traditions: Learn about the laws and customs of Egypt. Observe customs of the community and dress modestly when you attend places of worship.

2. Personal Safety: Protect Your Property: Pickpockets should be avoided, especially in busy places and marketplaces. Wear money belts and anti-theft pouches to protect your possessions.

• Be Aware: Be mindful of your surroundings at all times, especially in tourist destinations. Watch out for your personal property and be wary of con artists.

3. Health and Hygiene: • Food and Water: Choose your restaurants carefully, and drink bottled water. To avoid contracting foodborne infections, stay away from eating raw or peeled fruits and vegetables from street vendors.

Prescriptions: If you take prescription drugs, make sure you always have a sufficient quantity on hand as well as a duplicate of your prescriptions. Look into the availability of drugs in Egypt.

• Sun Protection: Egypt experiences hot, sunny days. Put on sunscreen, sunglasses, and proper clothing to protect oneself from the sun.

4. Transportation Safety:

- Licensed Transportation: For safe city transportation, use ride- sharing services like Uber or registered taxis. Before you go, make sure the meter is working or settle on the fare.
- Domestic Travel: Make sure you arrive at the airport well in advance and adhere to all security protocols while traveling domestically.

5. Tourist Attractions:
- Guided Tours: Take into account guided tours, particularly when going to less frequented locations. They provide additional security and provide local information.
- Honor Monuments: Show consideration for historical locations and relics. Refrain from climbing or touching historic buildings.

6. COVID-19 Points to Remember:
- Verification Needs: Keep up of COVID-19 recommendations, which may include

immunization, testing, and quarantine specifications. Observe local health regulations. With confidence, you may enjoy your trip to Egypt if you heed these travel safety advice. While staying secure is important, you shouldn't let it get in the way of discovering Egypt's rich history, culture, and natural beauty.

Healthcare And Emergency Contacts In Egypt

Major Egyptian cities offer high-quality healthcare thanks to state-of-the-art facilities and highly qualified medical staff. But it's crucial to be ready for any medical emergencies that may arise during your vacation. What you should know about emergency contacts and medical care in Egypt is as follows:

Medical Institutions:

1. Hospitals: There are contemporary medical facilities and English-speaking staff at hospitals in major towns including Sharm El Sheikh, Alexandria, and Cairo. As-Salaam International Hospital in Cairo and Al Salam International Hospital in Sharm El Sheikh are two of the well-known hospitals.

2. Clinics and Pharmacies: Egypt is home to a large number of pharmacies. There are clinics and medical facilities to offer basic healthcare services in towns and popular tourist destinations.

Health Guard Measures:

1. immunizations: Before visiting Egypt, find out if any immunizations are advised or necessary. Typhoid, hepatitis A, and regular vaccinations are examples of common vaccinations. For individualized advice, speaking with a healthcare professional is advised.

2. Water and Food Safety: To prevent foodborne infections, stick to bottled water and steer clear of undercooked or unpeeled fruits and vegetables from street vendors.

3. Sun Protection: To prevent sunburn, wear protective clothing, sunscreen, and sunglasses in Egypt because the country's sun is known for its intensity.

Emergency Numbers:

1. Medical Emergencies: Dial 123 if you have a medical emergency.

2. Police and General crises: Dial 122 for general crises or police assistance.

3. Fire and Rescue: Dial 180 in the event of a fire or other emergency needing rescue assistance.

4. Tourist Police: In popular tourist destinations, there are Tourist Police on duty. They can aid tourists with a variety of situations, such as reporting theft or getting assistance.

5. Consulates and Embassies: Find out the phone number and address of the embassy or consulate of your nation in Egypt. In the event of a passport issue or other consular concern, they can help.

Travel insurance :

Think about getting comprehensive travel insurance before your vacation. This ought to include lost property, canceled trips, and medical situations. When traveling, make sure you carry copies of your insurance and contact details.

You can guarantee a safe and happy trip to Egypt by being informed on healthcare services, emergency contacts, and basic health measures.

Even though most travelers are unlikely to need emergency medical attention, it's always a good idea to be ready.

Healthy Precautions And Vaccinations

Travelers arranging a vacation to Egypt must take health measures and vaccines into account. A safe and healthy visit can be ensured by taking the appropriate safety measures. What you should know is as follows:

Health Guard Measures:

1. Water and Food Safety: Although most big cities have chlorinated their tap water, it's still suggested to consume bottled water to lower your chance of stomach problems. When consuming street food, exercise caution, particularly in places where sanitation standards are dubious. Eat hot, freshly prepared meals to prevent foodborne infections, and stay away from unpeeled or undercooked produce from street sellers.

2. Sun Protection: Sun protection is essential because Egypt's weather may be hot and sunny. To prevent sunburn on your skin, use sunglasses, use sunscreen with a high SPF, and dress correctly.

3. Water intake: Drink plenty of water, particularly in dry areas and in hot weather. Keep a reusable water bottle with you and fill it up with bottled water as the day goes on.

4. Insect precautions: You may come with mosquitoes in some places, such as the Nile Delta, which can spread diseases like malaria. During the evenings and nights, think about donning long sleeves and applying insect repellent.

Immunizations:

1. Regular Immunizations: Make sure that all of your regular immunizations, including varicella, DTaP (diphtheria, tetanus, and pertussis), and MMR (measles, mumps, and rubella), are current.

2. Hepatitis A: Since tainted food and water can spread the virus, most visitors to Egypt are advised to get this vaccination.

3. Typhoid: Vaccination against typhoid is recommended, especially if you intend to travel to rural or less developed parts of Egypt where there may be issues with food and water hygiene. 4. Hepatitis B: If you want to remain a long time or expect to interact closely with the locals, you should think about being vaccinated against hepatitis B.

5. Rabies: Take into consideration getting vaccinated against rabies if your trip plans may expose you to animals, such as dogs.

6. Polio: Your healthcare professional may advise the polio vaccine based on your immunization history and the particular places you intend to visit.

7. Malaria: Malaria is primarily a seasonal disease that only spreads to specific regions, such as the Nile Delta. Whether or whether you require antimalarial medication may depend on your vacation itinerary and the season. See your healthcare practitioner or a travel medicine specialist for advice.

Consult a travel medicine specialist or your healthcare practitioner at least 4-6 weeks before your trip to Egypt. They can offer tailored advice depending on your condition, your itinerary, and the places you want to see. Taking these health measures and receiving the necessary vaccines will make your trip to Egypt safer and more enjoyable.

Responsible tourism in Egypt

In addition to taking in Egypt's breathtaking natural beauty and rich historical legacy, responsible tourism also aims to protect the ecological and cultural legacy of the nation for coming generations.

The following are some essential guidelines and procedures for ethical travel to Egypt:

1. Honor Local Traditions: Egypt is a conservative nation with a strong Islamic heritage. When visiting places of worship, dress modestly and take note of regional traditions. Prior to shooting pictures of someone, especially in a remote region, get their consent.

2. Preserve Historical Sites: Egypt is home to several of the most famous historical sites in the entire globe. As you explore these treasures, pay attention to what your tour guides are telling you and abide by the regulations about taking pictures and handling the antiques. Defacement, including graffiti, is strictly forbidden.

3. Encourage Local Communities: To boost the Egyptian economy, look for regional establishments and experiences. Select local tour guides, book lodging from nearby establishments, and purchase trinkets made by regional artists. This makes it possible to guarantee that local communities gain from the tourism sector.

4. Environmental Responsibilities: Be mindful of the surroundings when you're there. Don't litter, and be sure to properly dispose of any rubbish you bring with you. Due to the delicate ecosystems of some natural areas—such as the coral reefs in the Red Sea—responsible diving and snorkeling techniques are essential.

5. Water Conservation: Water is an extremely valuable resource in Egypt. Water should be used carefully, particularly in dry areas. To save water and energy, repurpose the towels and linens in your lodging.

6. Encounters with Wildlife: If you intend to travel to areas where you may come into contact with wildlife, keep a respectful distance and heed the advice of competent tour operators. Don't feed or bother animals.

7. Minimize Single-Use Plastic: Steer clear of single-use plastics like straws and bags and instead bring a reusable water bottle. The infrastructure for managing waste is inadequate in many places.

8. Cultural Awareness: Learn about the historical and cultural relevance of the locations you are visiting. Gaining an understanding of the background will improve your experience and show that you respect the location.

9. Pick Up a Few Arabic words: Although many Egyptians working in the tourism sector understand English, it can still be a sign of respect for the local way of life to know a few simple Arabic words.

10. Responsible Diving and Snorkeling: If you intend to explore the underwater environment of the Red Sea, make sure you abide by the rules on responsible diving and snorkeling, which include not handling or gathering marine species.

In Egypt, environmentally friendly travel is advantageous to visitors as well as to nearby communities. Following these guidelines will allow you to have fun on your vacation and make a constructive contribution to the nation and its citizens. Traveling responsibly guarantees that Egypt's natural beauty and cultural legacy are available to upcoming traveler generations.

Eco- Friendly Practices In Egypt

Egypt must adopt eco-friendly policies in order to protect its natural beauty and lessen the negative effects of tourism on the environment. The following eco-friendly policies and programs can aid in advancing sustainability:

1. Cut Down on Plastic Waste: Steer clear of single-use plastics like bags and water bottles. Use the reusable water bottle you brought with you the entire journey. Even in isolated places, dispose of your trash properly.

2. Conserve Water: Water is scarce in Egypt, thus water conservation is crucial. Reuse towels and linens during your stay, report leaky taps in your lodging, and use water sparingly.

3. Pick Responsible Tour Operators: Pick tour companies that are dedicated to sustainable and ethical travel. Seek out businesses that give back to the community, preserve the environment, and have minimal carbon footprints.

4. Encourage Local Businesses: Purchase trinkets and goods from regional producers and marketplaces.

Encourage the patronage of nearby eateries, lodging facilities, and enterprises to bolster the local economy.

5. Respect Coral Reefs: Take care not to touch or harm coral reefs when diving or snorkeling in the Red Sea. Respect the guidelines and responsible diving procedures to preserve this delicate habitat.

6. Take Part in Clean-Up Activities: If there are any scheduled or local beach and dive site clean-ups during your vacation, sign up to participate. Making a contribution to environmental conservation programs is a fulfilling way to support your neighborhood.

7. Educate Yourself: Get familiar with Egypt's environmental issues, such as waste management and water scarcity. You may plan your visit more wisely if you are aware of the local context.

8. Select Sustainable Accommodations: Seek out eco-friendly lodging establishments that employ eco-friendly techniques including conserving electricity and water, cutting back on trash, and utilizing renewable energy sources.

9. Take Public transit: To lessen your carbon impact in cities, choose public transit like buses and trams. Egypt's cities are frequently crowded, so taking public transportation can be a more environmentally friendly option.

10. Show Respect for Wildlife: Keep your distance from animals and report any examples of the illegal wildlife trade. Support the conservation of animals by going to reputable sanctuaries or reserves.

11. Encourage Renewable Energy: Egypt is investing much on solar power and other renewable energy sources. Opt for lodgings that use wind or solar power if at all possible.

12. Educational Experiences: Take into account ecotourism opportunities that advance environmental education and awareness. Numerous parks and reserves provide guided tours with an emphasis on conservation initiatives.

You may contribute to Egypt's tourism industry's sustainability and help preserve the country's natural environment by adopting these eco-friendly behaviors while you're there. By working together, we can guarantee that Egypt's extraordinary landscapes and cultural treasures will be accessible to future generations.

Activities For Families And Children

Egypt is a great place for a special family holiday because it has a large variety of family-friendly activities and attractions. The following are a few of Egypt's top family-friendly activities:

1. See the Pyramids and Sphinx: Stroll around the famous Giza Plateau and take in the sight of the Great Sphinx and the Pyramids of Giza. Kids will be in awe of these historic buildings' magnificence.

2. Mummies and History: See a vast array of items, including mummies and treasures from ancient Egypt, by visiting the Egyptian Museum in Cairo. For kids, it's an engaging and instructive experience.

3. Nile Felucca Ride: Take a traditional felucca for a leisurely trip down the Nile River.

The whole family may take in the picturesque splendor of the river and its surroundings during this leisurely activity.

4. Luxor Temple and Karnak Temple: Tour the expansive Karnak Temple complex as well as the Luxor Temple. Both adults and children will find the amazing architecture and hieroglyphics fascinating.

5. Nile River Cruises: Take into consideration a family-friendly Nile River cruise, which provides a cozy and picturesque approach to discover Egypt's historical treasures while taking use of contemporary conveniences.

6. Red Sea Adventures: For family-friendly aquatic pursuits like swimming and snorkeling in the pristine seas, visit the Red Sea shoreline. Hurghada and Sharm El Sheikh are well-liked travel spots.

7. Desert Adventures: Discover Egypt's breathtaking desert vistas by going on a family desert safari. In the dunes, kids can go camel riding and sandboarding.

8. Coptic Cairo: Take a tour of the ancient churches and discover the early Christian history of Egypt in this historic region of Cairo.

9. Children's Museums: A few Egyptian towns, such as Cairo, have kid-friendly museums with engaging activities and interactive displays for young minds.

10. Aquariums and Zoos: Children can view a variety of marine life and animals in aquariums and zoos located in Alexandria and other large cities.

11. Sound and Light Shows: A number of ancient landmarks, such as the Karnak Temple and the Pyramids of Giza, have amazing nighttime sound and light displays that offer families an enjoyable and instructive experience.

12. Bazaar shopping: Take your kids to local markets and bazaars to introduce them to the colorful street life, spices, and handicrafts of Egypt.

For families traveling with kids, Egypt's fascinating history, breathtaking natural scenery, and kid-friendly sites provide the ideal balance of adventure and education. It's a chance to instill in young brains a passion of culture and discovery as well as to make enduring memories.

kid-Friendly Attractions In Egypt

Egypt is an amazing travel destination for families with kids since it is full of historical marvels and cultural riches. Although many of Egypt's attractions are appropriate for children, the following kid-friendly choices are tailored especially for younger visitors:

1. Giza Zoo: The Giza Zoo, which is situated in Cairo, is home to a range of creatures, including monkeys, giraffes, and lions. Kids can have a great day exploring and seeing nature.

2. Dream Park: Located on 6th of October City, close to Cairo, this theme park has a variety of rides and kid-friendly activities. A fun-filled day full of entertainment alternatives awaits you.

3. Children's Civilization and Creativity Center: This Heliopolis-based facility offers hands- on activities and exhibits that captivate children while they learn about Egypt's natural world, history, and culture.

4. Magic Galaxy: Located in Cairo, this indoor amusement center has a roller rink, laser tag, arcade games, and other activities suitable for the whole family.

5. Science facilities in Cairo: Children can learn about science through interactive displays at a number of science facilities in Cairo, including the Science City and the Planetarium Science Center.

6. St. Katherine Butterfly Garden: Located on the Sinai Peninsula, this butterfly garden is a magical spot for kids to see different kinds of butterflies in their natural environment.

7. Pharaonic Village: This historical theme park in Giza provides an insight into ancient Egypt. Children can get a taste of pharaonic daily life and customs.

8. Alexandria Aquarium: The aquatic life on display here comes from the Red Sea, the Mediterranean Sea, and the Nile River. For younger guests, it's an enjoyable and instructive experience.

9. Children's Museums: There are children's museums in a few Egyptian cities that offer interactive displays and games meant to pique young children's interest and inventiveness.

10. Felucca Rides on the Nile: A peaceful and beautiful experience, a felucca ride on the Nile in Cairo is great for the whole family. Along the riverbanks, kids can see native lifestyles.

11. Mena House grounds: The Mena House Hotel, which is close to the Giza Pyramids, has beautifully landscaped grounds with breathtaking views of the pyramids. It is a nice area for a family walk.

12. Luna Park, Alexandria: This family-friendly amusement park in Alexandria offers rides, games, and other attractions.

Egypt offers children a variety of instructive and exciting experiences due to its numerous attractions; history, culture, and adventure combine to create a place where families may make lifelong memories.

Chapter 9 :

Solo Travel In Egypt

For your trip to Egypt to be fulfilling and worry-free, you must make sure you are safe and in good health. In Egypt, keep the following points in mind for your health and safety:

Security:

1. Personal belongings: Pay attention to what you own, particularly in busy places and popular tourist destinations. To stop theft, use money belts and secure baggage.

2. Local Customs: Learn about Egyptian etiquette and customs. When attending places of worship, dress modestly and follow local customs.

3. Guided Tours: Take into account guided tours for your safety and to learn about the place, particularly while visiting less-traveled locations.

4. Health Safety Measures: To prevent contracting a foodborne illness, exercise caution when buying food or beverages from street sellers. Refrain from drinking raw or peeled fruits and vegetables and stick to bottled water.

Wellness:

1. vaccines: Find out if any vaccines are necessary or advised before visiting Egypt. Typhoid, hepatitis A, and regular vaccinations are examples of common vaccinations.

2. Travel Insurance: Take into account getting travel insurance that includes coverage for both medical emergencies and trip disruptions or cancellations.

3. Sun Protection: To prevent sunburn, wear protective clothing, sunscreen, and sunglasses in

Egypt because the country's sun is known for its intensity.

4. Hydration: Maintain adequate hydration, particularly in arid areas and during hot weather. Opt for bottled water instead of tap water or ice in your beverages.

5. Medical Facilities: There are contemporary hospitals and medical facilities in large cities like Cairo and Alexandria. For minor medical emergencies, it is important to have a basic medical kit on hand.

6. Prescription Drugs: Make sure you have enough prescription drugs for your trip if you need them. Keep a copy of your prescriptions with you, and find out whether these drugs are available in Egypt.

7. Egyptian Cuisine: Although street food is generally tasty, be cautious when attempting it, particularly if you have a sensitive stomach.

8. Guidelines for COVID-19: Keep yourself informed about any changes to the COVID-19 rules, since they may involve testing and quarantine restrictions. Observe local health regulations.

around prudent safety and health measures, you can maximize your experience traveling around Egypt while lowering your risk. Like any travel destination, the secret to a safe and happy trip is to be well-informed and prepared.

Solo Travel Tips And Safety In Egypt

Egypt can be a fascinating and interesting place to visit, but as with any place, safety should always come first. The following travel safety advice may help you have a hassle-free and joyful trip to Egypt:

1. Planning and Research:

• Verify Travel Warnings: Examine the safety instructions and travel advisories that your government's foreign affairs department has provided before your trip. This will update you on Egypt's current state of affairs.

• Travel Insurance: Invest in all-inclusive travel insurance that includes coverage for lost luggage, medical emergencies, and trip cancellations. Make sure you have copies of your policy and your contact details on hand in case you require help.

• Regional Laws and Traditions: Learn about the laws and customs of Egypt. Observe customs of the community and dress modestly when you attend places of worship.

2. Personal Safety: Protect Your Property: Pickpockets should be avoided, especially in busy places and marketplaces. Wear money belts and anti-theft pouches to protect your possessions. Stay Alert: Pay close attention to your surroundings at all times, especially in tourist destinations. Watch out for your personal property and be wary of con artists.

3. Health and Hygiene:

- Food and Water: Choose your restaurants carefully, and drink bottled water. To avoid contracting foodborne infections, stay away from eating raw or peeled fruits and vegetables from street vendors.

Prescriptions: If you take prescription drugs, make sure you always have a sufficient quantity on hand as well as a duplicate of your prescriptions. Look into the availability of drugs in Egypt.

- Sun Protection: Egypt experiences hot, sunny days. Put on sunscreen, sunglasses, and proper clothing to protect oneself from the sun.

4. Safety of Transportation:

- Transportation Under License: For safe city transportation, use ride-sharing services like Uber or authorized taxis. Before you go, make sure the meter is working or settle on the fare.

- Domestic Travel: Make sure you arrive at the airport well in advance and adhere to all security protocols while traveling domestically.

5. Tourist Attractions:

- Guided Tours: Take into account guided tours, particularly when going to less frequented locations. They provide additional security and provide local information.

- Honor Monuments: Show consideration for historical locations and relics. Refrain from climbing or touching historic buildings.

6. COVID-19 Points to Remember:

- Verification Needs: Keep up of COVID-19 recommendations, which may include immunization, testing, and quarantine specifications. Observe local health regulations.

With confidence, you may enjoy your trip to Egypt if you heed these travel safety advice. While staying secure is important, you shouldn't let it get in the way of discovering Egypt's rich history, culture, and natural beauty.

Meeting local And Fellow Travelers in Egypt:

Having conversations with Egyptians and other tourists can improve your trip by giving you a deeper understanding of the country's culture and fostering lifelong friendships. Here are a few strategies for making new friends when exploring Egypt:

1. Visit Local Markets: You can interact with residents and businesses by meandering around crowded souks and markets, such as Khan el-Khalili in Cairo. Never be afraid to start a discussion and discover more about their customs and arts.

2. Take Part in Guided trips: Group trips to historical locations such as the Pyramids or the Temples of Luxor offer a chance to network with other tourists. Making new friends might result from sharing experiences with others.

3. Take Part in Local Events: Look into any festivals, cultural gatherings, or musical events that are scheduled for the time you will be there. These are great chances to meet people and discover more about Egyptian customs.

4. Visit Cafes and Restaurants: Take a tour of the neighborhood's cafes and restaurants to sample the delicious Egyptian food and strike up a discussion with the amiable residents. Egyptians are renowned for their cordial welcome.

5. Language Exchange: Take into account language exchange programs or applications that pair you up with Egyptians who want to practice their English if you're attempting to study Arabic or just want to interact with locals.

6. Stay in Hostels: Choose hostels in well-known tourist locations like Aswan, Luxor, and Cairo to meet other lone travelers in common areas. There, you may exchange stories and possibly even form travel companions.

7. Online Travel Communities: To meet and connect with other travelers or foreigners residing in Egypt, sign up for online travel forums, social media groups, or applications like Meetup.

8. Attend Workshops or Classes: To meet others who share your interests, take part in art, cooking, or workshop sessions in your community.

9. Couchsurfing and Homestays: Take into account possibilities like couchsurfing or homestays, which let you live with locals and learn more about Egyptian culture.

10. Volunteer: There are plenty of opportunities to make a difference while interacting with locals and other volunteers from abroad when you volunteer in Egypt.

Egyptians are renowned for their warmth and hospitality, and they frequently want to talk to visitors. Through engaging in many activities and delving into the local culture, you can forge bonds that will enhance your trip to Egypt and give you a more profound understanding of this amazing nation.

Travel Apps And Online Tools

Your trip to Egypt can be substantially improved by using online resources and travel apps, which make it easier for you to get around, locate information, and maintain connections. For your journey to Egypt, here are some must-have travel applications and internet resources:

1. Google Maps: An excellent navigational tool is Google Maps. You may see nearby companies, get directions, and get up-to-date traffic data. Get maps to utilize offline in the event that you come across places with spotty internet access.

2. Uber: Uber serves as a practical and dependable form of transportation in Egypt's largest cities, including Cairo and Alexandria.

Comparing it to regular taxis, it's frequently more transparent and safer.

3. Booking.com and Airbnb: These websites provide a variety of lodging options, including hotels, flats, and homestays. You can pursue evaluations and reserve lodging that fits your needs and price range.

4. Tripadvisor: If you're looking for advice, ratings, and reviews for Egyptian hotels, eateries, and tourist sites, Tripadvisor is a helpful tool. It might assist you in choosing wisely what to pack for your trip.

5. Duolingo: This user-friendly language study program can be useful if you wish to learn or practice some basic Arabic phrases before your trip.

6. XE Currency Converter: Use the XE Currency Converter app or website to quickly convert local currency—the Egyptian

Pound—into your home currency and to remain up to current on exchange rates.

7. Egypt e-Visa Portal: You can finish the online application process if you need to apply for a visa before your trip by using the official Egypt e-Visa portal.

8. Wi-Fi Finder Apps: To find free Wi-Fi hotspots in Egypt, especially in urban areas, download Wi-Fi finder apps like Wi-Fi Map or Instabridge.

9. Ride-Sharing Apps: In addition to Uber, you may want to look into regional ride-sharing services like Careem, which function in Egyptian cities and provide a substitute for conventional taxis.

10. EgyptAir App: This app might be useful for booking domestic flights, tracking the status of your flight, and getting travel information if you intend to fly within Egypt.

11. Apps for Currency Exchange Rates: Use apps such as CurrencyConverter Plus to stay up to date on exchange rates. This can help you make wise financial decisions while traveling.

12. Weather applications: Use weather applications like AccuWeather or The Weather Channel to stay up to date on the local weather in Egypt.

Before your journey to Egypt, make sure you download and become familiar with these travel applications and online resources. They can assist you in making the most of your trip by making sure you have easy access to vital information, can travel the nation without difficulty, and can maintain contact with friends and family back home.

Maps and Navigation

Many map and navigation choices make it easy to navigate Egypt's historical monuments, busy cities, and desert landscapes. Here's how to navigate the nation efficiently:

1. Google Maps: One useful resource for traveling in Egypt is Google Maps. It provides thorough maps, walking, driving, and public transportation instructions, as well as up-to-date traffic information. To save on data costs, you can also download maps for offline use.

2. Ubers and careem: Major Egyptian cities including Cairo, Alexandria, and Sharm El Sheikh are home to a large user base of Uber and Careem, two ride-sharing applications. They offer quick and safe transit options, frequently at set prices.

3. GPS Devices: If you would rather not use your smartphone for navigation in Egypt, think about packing a small GPS gadget. Before your journey, make sure the device is updated with the most recent maps.

4. Local Taxis: In Egypt, traditional taxis are often used. Prior to beginning your trip, it's a good idea to negotiate a fare with the driver or make sure the meter is running.

5. Public Transportation: Buses, trams, and metro services are available in Egypt's largest cities, including Cairo and Alexandria. Think about requesting directions from locals or utilizing Google Maps.

6. Tour Guides: Having a local tour guide can be quite beneficial when visiting historical locations. They not only offer insightful commentary, but they also help you navigate challenging historical contexts.

7. Offline Maps: In addition to Google Maps, you can utilize specialized offline map applications such as Here WeGo or MAPS.ME. With the help of these programs, you can use offline maps of Egypt that you have previously downloaded.

8. Local Knowledge: When in Egypt, don't be afraid to ask people for directions. In general, Egyptians are amiable and eager to assist disoriented tourists. For communication purposes, picking up a few simple Arabic phrases might also be helpful.

9. Road Signs: If you intend to drive, familiarize yourself with Egyptian traffic laws and road signs. Major highways sometimes contain English signage in addition to the Arabic that is used for road signs.

10. Guided Tours: When visiting historical places, guided tours are a popular choice among travelers.

Tour operators typically set up vehicles and guides, which simplifies navigation.

11. Maps obtained through lodging: Local maps and assistance with directions and transit alternatives are frequently offered by hotels and other lodging establishments.

Equipped with the appropriate navigational aids, one can more easily explore Egypt's varied landscapes and historical treasures. You'll have little trouble navigating this fascinating nation, whether you use tour guides, digital maps, or local transportation.

Chapter 10 :

Language and Communicating

Egypt's rich cultural heritage and varied history have contributed to the country's distinct language and communication patterns. What you need know about communication and language in Egypt is as follows:

1. Official Language: Arabic is Egypt's official language. Particularly in daily life, Egyptian Arabic is commonly spoken. Even though the majority of Egyptians living in cities are somewhat conversant in English, Arabic is still the most often used language for communication.

2. Arabic Dialect: Egyptian Arabic is the particular dialect of Arabic spoken by Egyptians. The majority of Egyptians are able to transition between dialect and standard Arabic as needed, albeit it may differ from the standard Arabic you may have learned in language classes.

3. English Language: People who work in the tourism sector, stay in hotels, and visit tourist destinations frequently utilize English. English-speaking people are comparatively easy to locate in big towns like Luxor and Cairo.

4. Simple Arabic Phrases: Acquiring a few simple Arabic phrases, like salutations and courteous utterances, can be beneficial and well-received by the locals. When visitors attempt to speak Arabic, Egyptians will typically greet them with warmth.

5. Arabic writing: For individuals who are not familiar with the language, Arabic writing might be problematic because it reads from right to left. Arabic and English signage is common in large cities' road signs and public transportation systems.

6. bilingual signage: In tourist locations, especially historical monuments and lodgings, you could come across bilingual signage in addition to Arabic and English.

7. Non-Verbal Communication: Egyptians communicate a lot through non-verbal means. In daily talks and interactions, body language, facial expressions, and hand gestures are important.

8. Tipping Culture: Tipping, or "baksheesh," is customary in Egypt and tipping manners are subject to change. For interactions to go smoothly, especially in restaurants and service settings, it is imperative to know how much to tip and when.

9. Traveler Details: Staff members at significant historical sites and tourist information centers are typically fluent in English and other major languages and are available to assist visitors.

Even if Arabic is the native tongue in tourist locations, learning a few phrases in the language might improve your trip and make you more popular with the locals. Respecting their language and culture can result in more meaningful interactions with Egyptians during your visit, since they are generally kind and accommodating.

Essential Egyptian Phrases

Acquiring knowledge of a few fundamental Egyptian Arabic phrases will significantly improve your trip to Egypt. Although most people in tourist destinations speak English, trying to communicate in Arabic can be welcomed by the locals and lead to more genuine relationships. To help you get started, consider these important words:

1. Greetings:

- Hello: "Marhaba" (مرحبا)
- Good morning: "Sabah el-kheir" (صباح الخير)
- Good afternoon: "Masaa el-kheir" (مساء الخير)
- Good evening: "Masaa el-noor" (مساء النور)
- Goodbye: "Ma'a salama" (مع السلامة)

2. Politeness:

- Please: "Min fadlik" (من فضلك)
- Thank you: "Shukran" (شكرًا)
- You're welcome: "Afwan" (عفوًا)
- Excuse me / I'm sorry: "Asif" (آسف)
- Yes: "Na'am" (نعم)
- No: "La" (لا)

3. Asking for Help:

- Can you help me?: "Momkin mosa'ada?" (ممكن مساعدة؟)
- I'm lost: "Dai'ait" (ضاعيت)
- Where is...?: "Fein...?" (فين...؟)
- How much is this?: "Kam da?" (كام ده؟)

4. Basic Numbers:

- One: "Waahid" (واحد)
- Two: "Ithnaan" (اثنان)
- Three: "Talata" (ثلاثة)
- Four: "Arbaa" (أربعة)
- Five: "Khamsa" (خمسة)

5. Food and Dining:

- Menu: "El-qeemat" (القائمة)
- Water: "Ma'a" (ماء)
- I would like...: "Ana 'ayez..." (أنا عايز...)
- The check, please: "El-hesab, min fadlik" (الحساب، من فضلك)

6. Directions:

- Where is the bathroom?: "Fein el-hammam?" (فين الحمام؟)
- Right: "Yameen" (يمين)
- Left: "Shemaal" (شمال)
- Straight ahead: "Wahtdhu ala tool" (واحدا على طول)

7. Common Phrases:

- I don't understand: "Ana mish fahem" (أنا مش فاهم)
- What is your name?: "Ismak eh?" (اسمك إيه؟)
- I'm a tourist: "Ana saffar" (أنا سائح)
- Help!: "I'mdaad!" (إمداد!)

Whether you're placing an order for food, getting directions, or just being kind, these fundamental phrases will come in useful in daily conversations. In general, Egyptians are likely to react favorably to foreigners who attempt to speak Arabic. Keep in mind to speak in a courteous manner, and don't give up if you make mistakes—locals are frequently understanding and grateful for your efforts.

Cultural Insight and Etiquette

It is essential to comprehend Egyptian customs and etiquette in order to travel in this multicultural and historically rich nation with grace and enjoyment. The following are some salient cultural insights and manners advice:

1. Respect for Islam: Since Islam is the most common religion in Egypt, Islamic principles are deeply ingrained in daily life. Show consideration for regional traditions and customs. It is traditional to pause and pay respect during the Islamic call to prayer, known as Adhan.

During these periods, refrain from talking loudly or interjecting.

2. Modesty in Attire:

- Wear modest attire, particularly when you visit places of worship. Women ought to conceal their knees, cleavage, and shoulders. Moreover, men ought to refrain from donning shorts and sleeveless shirts in these settings. Beachwear is exclusively suitable for beach resorts. In some contexts, modest clothing is valued.

3. Salutations:

- "As-salamu alaykum" (peace be upon you) is the traditional Arabic greeting. "Wa alaykum as-salam" is the reply (and upon you be peace). "Marhaba" (hello) is a typical Egyptian Arabic greeting.

4. Expressing Love:

- In Egypt, it is usually considered inappropriate to show love in public. It's best not to give hugs, kisses, or handshakes to strangers.

5. Elders and Respect:

- Egyptian society places a high value on showing respect for the elderly. When conversing with senior citizens, be kind and respectful.

6. Tipping (Baksheesh):

- In Egypt, tipping, or "baksheesh," is customary. Always remember to leave a tip for servers, particularly at dining establishments, lodgings, and when you get help. Tipping plays a big role in the local economy.

7. Bargaining:

- In markets and souks, bargaining is customary. It's normal to haggle over pricing when shopping. Negotiate with assertiveness and politeness.

8. Removing Shoes:
- It is traditional to take off your shoes when you enter a house, so be ready to do so if you are invited over.

9. Left Hand Use:

- In Arab culture, the left hand is typically regarded as less hygienic. It's customary to eat, give and receive objects, and greet people with your right hand.

10. Queuing:

- In crowded public areas, be ready for disorganized lines. It's possible that people don't always obey rules.

11. Photography:

- When shooting pictures of people, especially in rural regions, always get their permission.

Although most Egyptians are willing to oblige, it is polite to ask first.

Travelers who identify as female should take extra care, particularly if they are going alone. It's best to dress modestly and pay attention to your surroundings.

You may establish good relations with the locals and guarantee a more uneventful, courteous, and pleasurable trip to Egypt by adhering to these cultural insights and etiquette recommendations.

Egyptians are typically friendly and grateful when visitors demonstrate an awareness of their customs and culture.

Final Though

In summary, Egypt is an enthralling and diverse tourism destination where the past and contemporary coexist harmoniously. Travelers will find this country to be a dream because of its abundance of historical wonders and breathtaking natural scenery, which ranges from the majesty of the Pyramids to the peace of the Nile River.

Egypt's illustrious past, spanning millennia, has permanently impacted the global landscape. The breathtaking accomplishments of the ancient Egyptian civilization are demonstrated by the Great Pyramids of Giza, the Temples of Luxor, and the Valley of the Kings. These enormous constructions are breathtaking and compel us to consider the creativity of their builders.

Egypt's modernity, with its thriving marketplaces, friendly populace, and busy cities, stands in stark contrast to its ancient history. Egypt today is a modern nation that values its history while thriving in the present, as evidenced by the urban life and cultural fusion found in cities like Alexandria and Cairo.

Another element of magic to Egypt is added by the Nile River, which is sometimes referred to be the country's lifeblood.

It is an experience that will last a lifetime to cruise this historic waterway, see rural life along its banks, and explore the ancient temples that border its shores. Egypt's food tantalizes the senses with its mouth watering variety of flavors, ranging from street food to gourmet treats. It's a must to sample foods like falafel, koshari, and aromatic teas along the way.

Egypt provides a wonderful combination of educational opportunities and adventures for families. Experiencing history from the eyes of youngsters, investigating historic graves, and navigating busy marketplaces leave a lasting impression.

For lone travelers, safety is paramount, and Egypt has a friendly atmosphere as long as you take the appropriate safety measures and behave thoughtfully.

Positive relationships can be greatly facilitated by showing respect for regional traditions and learning a little Arabic.

Egypt promises an experience unlike any other, a place where culture dances in the streets, history whispers in the winds, and the Nile nurtures life. You add to Egypt's rich tapestry as you stroll through the historic temples, savor regional food, and feel the kindness of the populace.

Discover its mysteries and go on an exploration of the land of the Pharaohs. Egypt offers a voyage that will make an enduring impression on your heart and spirit, whether your goal is to experience the magnificence of ancient civilization or the vibrancy of modern life.

Printed in Great Britain
by Amazon